LESBIANS TALK MAKING BLACK WAVES

LESBIANS TALK

Making Black Waves

Valerie Mason-John
and Ann Khambatta

Scarlet Press

Acknowledgments

We would like to thank everyone who has contributed to this book, in particular those women who have spoken to us personally and all those who sent back questionnaires. A special thankyou to Dorothea Smartt and Savitri Hensman for reading the manuscript and for their responses. We would also like to thank Nasreen Memon and Out on a Limb for their help in compiling the filmography. Many thanks to Belinda Budge and Vicky Wilson from Scarlet Press for their invaluable support in making this book a reality. Thanks also to Zehra and Nina Rapi for allowing us to use the 'Lesbians from Historically Immigrant Communities' research materials. We would also like to thank Women and Manual Trades and the Black Lesbian and Gay Centre for the use of their resources. Thanks to Account 3, Gemma Mars and Yael Hodder for their administrative and design support and to Caroline Kerslake and Char Scrivener for their photographic and printing skills.

Valerie I would like to extend thanks to the women in my life who have always believed in me, my foster mother Carol Gallaghar, chosen sister Shirley Henry, friends Suzanne Roden, Zenobi Bynoe, Lorna Lee Leslie, Pat Adams and my lover Alex Tagg. And to young Carol James, who kept me on my toes and up to date with the scene, and her partner Dawn Thibert. Finally, I would like to thank my co-writer Ann for her support, trust and honest discussions.

Ann I would like to thank Valerie for her trust in me and the process, her honesty and patience. You'll be a hard act to follow. Thankyou to Adrian and Katrina for their grounding and youthful insights into the world's adultism and the real need for Fun. Thanks also to Teresa for her insight and recognition of the need for home truths. Finally, many, many thanks to Anna, my mum Erika and brother Andy for their belief in emotional honesty and love of self as integral to creating true bridges of understanding between us.

Published by Scarlet Press, 5 Montague Road, London E8 2HN

Copyright © Valerie Mason-John and Ann Khambatta 1993

British Library Cataloguing-in-Publication Data
A catalogue record for this book is available from the British Library
ISBN 1 85727 007 X

All rights reserved. No part of this publication may be reproduced or transmitted in any form or by any means, electronic or mechanical, including photocopy, recording, or any information storage and retrieval system, without permission in writing from the publisher

Series editors: Belinda Budge and Vicky Wilson
Cover design: Pat Kahn
Typesetting: Kathryn Holliday
Printed in Great Britain

Contents

9   Introduction

11   We have always been here

19   Out and about

26   Separate worlds

32   Black: whose term is it anyway?

38   If the label fits, wear it

45   Racism in the margins

50   SM politics

52   Fast-forward

56   Now and then: a Black lesbian chronology

60   Resources
Groups and contacts 60
Further reading 61
Film and video 62

Abbreviations used in this book are as follows:
(QR): questionnaire respondent
(LHIC): Lesbians from Historically Immigrant Communities
(LHIC is a collection of interviews conducted during the mid 1980s)
B: born
P: parents

About the authors

Valerie Mason-John and **Ann Khambatta** have both been active and visible in the Black lesbian community since the early 1980s. This is the first writing project on which they have collaborated together.

Valerie Mason-John has worked for the national, Black, feminist and lesbian and gay press in Britain, and is one of the collective editors of *Feminist Arts News (FAN)*. She has also worked as a freelance researcher for BBC television and radio, Channel 4's *Out* series and the Arts Council of Great Britain. She is currently the lesbian listings reporter for Spectrum radio's late night show *G.A.Y.* and is studying at the Desmond Jones School of Physical Theatre and Mime. She is exploring her creativity through performing, film-making and writing short stories and poetry. B: England. I am Black British from the African Diaspora, and was transracially placed in Dr Barnardos and White foster homes.

Ann Khambatta has worked in the London voluntary sector in a paid and unpaid capacity for the past nine years. She has worked for the Black Lesbian and Gay Centre and other Black, lesbian and gay and women's organisations in a variety of capacities: as a community accountant, fundraiser, administrator and trainer. She was a member of the collective for *Outwrite Women's Newspaper* and since it folded in 1989 she has regularly contributed articles to the lesbian and gay and women's press. She is currently researching her parents' histories and exploring the creative possibilities of wielding a needle and thread. B: England. I am of Indian Parsee and German descent. I was brought up by my German mother.

Contributors

Aqeela Alam is Asian, a counsellor and activist. B: Guyana P: Pakistan

Linda Bellos was leader of Lambeth Council between 1985 and 1987. She is a mother, and calls herself an independent thinker. B: England P: Nigeria/Polish-Russian Jew

Marlene Bogle was an advice worker at Brixton Black Women's Centre. She is a sexual-abuse counsellor. B: Jamaica P: Jamaica

Da Choong is a tired woman warrior searching for a new way to make sense of the world. B: Malaysia P: Fourth-generation Malaysian/China

Anne Hayfield has 14 years' experience of campaigning for the rights of women, Black people, lesbians and gay men. She currently describes herself as disillusioned in Dulwich. B: England P: African Caribbean/Asian

Anna Juleya Hearne is a philosopher and Woman of Colour of mixed racial heritage. Jamaican by birth, British by education and American by association.

Savitri Hensman, 31, lives in London. She writes poetry and since 1985 has worked for the Black Lesbian and Gay Centre as an outreach and development worker. B: Sri Lanka P: Sri Lanka

Teresa Hope is a burnt-out feminist activist, training to be a counsellor. B: Chile P: Chile

Jackie Kay was born and brought up in Scotland, is a writer and lives in London with her son. B: Scotland and identifies as Black Scottish

Hope Massiah was one of the organisers of the Zami II conference in 1989, and of Sauda – a group of women of African descent who organised social events for Black women – in 1992. She is the development manager of Positively Women. B: Barbados P: Barbados

Araba Mercer was involved in Manchester's Black Women's Group during the mid 1980s. She is a publisher for Sheba Feminist Publishers. B: Ghana P: Ghana/England

Madge was active on the London lesbian scene during the late 1960s and 70s. She is a mother living in London. B: Carriacou P: Carriacou

Marie is a mother and grandmother who has lived most of her life in England. She is independent, interested in Black and feminist issues and keen to meet other older Black lesbians. B: Barbados P: Barbados

Femi Otitoju was a volunteer with the national Lesbian and Gay Switchboard. She is director of Challenge, a training company in equality issues. B: Nigeria P: Nigeria (transracially placed with a White adoptive family)

Dorothea Smartt was one of the founders of the Black Lesbian Support Network in 1983. She is a Black arts co-ordinator and performance poet. B: England P: Barbados

Zehra is happy to have raised the issue of lesbian immigration and to have worked and campaigned around it. B: Turkey P: Crete/Macedonia

In Lesbians Talk Making Black Waves *we have written an account that is honest and so, at times, critical, both of Black lesbians and of the wider Black communities. This was not an easy decision to make in a society where we face marginalisation and discrimination. We have done this from a position of love; both of ourselves in all our complexities and for the potential of our communities. It is also with love that we send this book out into the world, as a testament to Black lesbians in Britain.*

Introduction

This is the first book to record the history of Black lesbians living in Britain and to discuss the main issues that have affected us during the past 15 years. We believe it marks an important political and cultural contribution to documenting our lives in this country.

The majority of books on Black lesbians are from the US. These have been of invaluable support to us in coming to terms with the effects of racism and homophobia and in helping us to strengthen and develop our lesbian identities. However, the herstories and experiences described within them are different from ours, and we have little written information on what the Black lesbian experience in Britain can provide. Our lives have occasionally been documented in sections of anthologies, but many of the newsletters and articles we have produced or contributed to have disappeared. The few relevant archives and libraries – the Black Lesbian and Gay Centre, Lesbian Archives and Feminist Library face threats to their future. It is therefore essential that we chronicle our achievements, struggles and debates before they are forgotten or disappear.

The research for this book was compiled from interviews with 16 Black lesbians, questionnaires distributed to Black lesbians living all over Britain, printed and oral herstories. The country of birth of every Black lesbian quoted and of her parents – where we have known these – are given as an important first step in documenting the many complex routes, both racial and geographical, by which we have arrived here.

While researching and writing this book, it was essential to define the term Black. In essence, the definition we have worked with is that of the London Black Lesbian and Gay Centre, namely, those:

descended (through one or both parents) from Africa, Asia (i.e. the Middle East to China, including the Pacific nations) and Latin America, and lesbians and gay men descended from the original inhabitants of Australasia, North America, and the islands of the Atlantic and Indian Ocean.

All these countries have at some time been subject to colonialism and imperialism. Black lesbians who originate from these countries have all experienced racism in Britain on both a personal and institutional level.

Our personal view of what are and have been important issues and discussions for Black lesbians is inevitably reflected in the choice of chapter subjects. Our experiences and Black identities are different: while one of us is of African descent with Black birth parents, the other is of Asian/German descent with Black and White birth parents. In order to cross this divide, discuss our differences and make sense of our experiences as Black lesbians within the lesbian, gay and heterosexual communities, we have made bridges from our similarities: of both having been brought up in Britain by White birth or foster parents. We recognise the fact that neither of us fits neatly into prevalent, one-dimensional notions of Black lesbian identity and have used this recognition to explore the assumptions and myths which have surrounded us and silenced the wealth of experiences and herstories our communities hold.

'Out and about' challenges the negative views of lesbians in both the Black and White communities by celebrating the existence of lesbians in some Black societies since 500AD. One of the more difficult chapters to write was 'Black: whose term is it anyway?' In it we explore some of the issues surrounding the word and look at how Black as an umbrella term has failed to include us all. 'If the label fits, wear it' looks at the diversity of labels we use to describe ourselves and how we have at times adapted these by adding the prefix Black or our countries of origin. This chapter also looks at terms which originate from the Caribbean and India – zami and khush respectively.

While it is by no means definitive, *Lesbians Talk Making Black Waves* is a beginning. We hope our readers will feel a glow of recognition at the sentiments and herstories contained in these pages and that many more books about, for and by Black lesbians living in Britain will be written.

We have always been here

There have been Black people in Britain for at least 500 years and for all that time there have been Black lesbians too. But isolation, racism and homophobia have made us invisible. In the last 15 to 20 years, Black lesbians have struggled to overcome this invisibility. We have organised groups and conferences, taken photographs of one another, filmed our lives and written about our experiences.

In the 1970s many Black lesbians were involved in militant Black groups, anti-racist and anti-fascist groups. Here personal issues such as sexuality were seen as unimportant in comparison with the greater political struggles against racism, fascism and capitalism. Other lesbians were part of the Women's Liberation Movement (WLM), where the emphasis on the universality of women's experience meant that the realities of race and racism were ignored. We were supposedly all women together, facing the same problems that were the result of male supremacy. There was no acceptance that oppression between women could exist, so racism was not seen as a women's issue.

Black women who were involved in the women's movement had a really rough time. I remember going to a women's meeting in 1978 and suggesting that we could create some international links and the women laughed, they laughed at me. Teresa Hope

On the whole, Black lesbians remained silent and isolated. We were required to break our identities into acceptable fragments: we were Black in Black groups, women in the women's movement and lesbians on the lesbian scene. There was no space to be whole, to be a Black lesbian.

By the end of the 1970s Black women were demanding that issues of race be addressed in the WLM and that issues of gender be addressed through the formation of separate caucuses within Black groups, anti-racist and anti-fascist groups. By 1978 a number of Black women's groups had sprung up across the country. OWAAD (Organisation of Women of African and Asian Descent) provided the first national forum for debate for some of those women.

Rise and fall of OWAAD

In February 1978 African women active in the African Students' Union in Britain launched what was known initially as the Organisation of Women of Africa and African Descent. After a series of meetings it was agreed that OWAAD should change its focus and it was renamed the Organisation of Women of African and Asian Descent, reflecting a decision to focus on those Black women here in Britain.

The first day-long conference in 1978 attracted 250 women. Speakers presented papers on a range of topics and there were also workshops. The women who attended were excited at sharing their experiences but felt there was not enough time or space, so it was agreed that this should become an annual event. In the meantime a newsletter (*FOWAAD*) and various committees were set up to keep women in touch with each other. By 1980 the OWAAD conference had grown to a two-day event attended by nearly 600 women. Issues discussed included Black women's organising within Black liberation struggles, Afro-Asian unity and the links between consciousness-raising and Black feminism.

During 1981 racist violence in Britain increased and tension between the police and the African-Caribbean and Asian communities reached breaking point. Riots occurred in many cities and towns throughout the country. At the 1981 OWAAD conference, women were incensed that in such a climate of hostility some women should consider a lesbian workshop to be important. Many participants felt that at a time such as this, issues of women's oppression and sexuality should be subordinate to the needs of the wider Black communities. Others were afraid that the accusation of being a lesbian would be thrown at them (Black men had frequently used this as a weapon against vocal Black women). But the lesbians calling for a workshop refused to be silenced. There was uproar. Insults like 'mash 'em up', 'chuck them out' and 'it's disgusting' were hurled at lesbian participants. Yet despite the hostility and anger, the lesbian workshop went ahead and kept filling up.

For the first five minutes we all looked at each other, sharing a real high, because there were so many of us, forty of us, there.
'Feminist Review', No.17, 1984

OWAAD never recovered from this split. Another conference took place in 1982 to try to save the organisation, but many women previously involved stayed away and many of the new women saw the theme of Black feminism as irrelevant to their lives.

Though the issue of lesbianism and sexuality in general had contributed to OWAAD's demise, there had been other sources of division. While in theory the need for African, African-Caribbean and Asian unity was recognised, in reality individuals and groups of women were far from united. This proved to be one of the fundamental flaws of the organisation.

The concept 'Black', had very different meanings for those of us living in white-dominated societies and regions, compared to those of us from societies which were ostensibly independent. 'Feminist Review', ibid

How could the main struggles be against racism and sexism when some African women's priorities included the liberation of their countries? OWAAD, despite its name change, was formed mainly of African and African-Caribbean women. Though supposedly politically all-embracing, in reality OWAAD did not represent Asian women's concerns.

The lesbian workshop at the 1981 conference had provided many Black lesbians with much-needed proof that they were not alone. As a result of this meeting Britain's first Black lesbian group was set up. The group was denied meeting space at Brixton Black Women's Centre in London because the workers felt they had enough problems from the community as a Black women's centre without the extra trouble they feared a lesbian group might bring. Eventually space was found at A Women's Place in London and 30 to 40 women regularly attended the fortnightly meetings, some from as far afield as Norwich and Scotland (a fares pool was established to help offset travel costs). Attended mainly by women of African descent, the group became a springboard for Black lesbian events in years to come.

Out with a vengeance

The early 1980s saw an explosion of events organised by and for Black lesbians. Most of these, though attended by women from all over the country, were held in London. Outside the capital, house parties called Blues, with a DJ, bar and doorcharge, were the only meeting places for many Black lesbians. Although particular to African-Caribbean culture, Blues were sometimes run and attended by other Black women.

There was very little for Black lesbians in Manchester during the early 1980s. There were mainly parties. A network of women travelled between Sheffield, Manchester and Leeds for parties. Araba Mercer

The Black Women and Media conference, held in April 1984, invited 'Black women and Women of Colour' to try their hand at practical workshops such as video-making, layout and design, and photography. Co-organised by *Outwrite Women's Newspaper*, the conference also provided space to discuss the representation of Black women in the media and ways to improve this. Lesbians were visible as organisers, facilitators and participants. A group of women later raised the issue of London-centric attitudes.

The same support network and resources do not exist for Black women outside London. Our experiences are sometimes very different and we don't feel this is acknowledged by Black women in London. So it becomes a London conference at which we are observers and we leave with a greater sense of isolation. 'Outwrite Women's Newspaper', Issue 25, 1984

The following month 250 women of African, African-Caribbean and Asian descent took part in the We Are Here: Black Feminists in Britain conference. Black lesbians were involved in the organisation, and it showed.

It was unashamedly a Black conference where Black lesbians were welcome. Dorothea Smartt

I remember on the Sunday there was an announcement – would all lesbians wanting to go to the Tea Dance leave now – and half the conference got up and left. Aqeela Alam

There were workshops for women of mixed race, and others on our differences, Black feminism and lesbians. The conference also produced a newsletter of the same name, and as a result of workshops and discussions a Black incest-survivors group and a mixed race women's group were set up. The event was marred by a debate on who was and was not Black, sparked off by women objecting to the presence of a light-skinned participant.

The first International Feminist Bookfair, held in London in June 1984, brought Black women from all over the globe to Britain to read and discuss their writing. Among these were Black lesbian authors Barbara Burford, Audre Lorde and Suniti Namjoshi. The last two were panel members at the International Lesbian Writers evening. The audience that night, as at most other bookfair events, was made up predominantly of White women. Audre Lorde refused to read until more Black women were allowed in.

In October 1985, Zami I, the first national Black lesbian conference, was held in London. Over 200 women of African-Caribbean and Asian descent attended. Zami I was an important landmark – the first time Black lesbians had come together in significant numbers to discuss a wide range of issues.

The previous year a Working Class Lesbian Weekend had been held in Leeds, funded by donations from White middle-class women. At the end of the weekend £11,000 remained and the women who attended agreed that this should go to Black lesbians to organise an event of their choice. However, £7,800 was stolen from the account by a couple of Black lesbians, so the donation was reduced to £3,000. This money funded Zami I.

The workshops at Zami I included Coming Out, bringing up children, incest, disability and our prejudices. But despite the initial joy of being together, divisions became apparent at the plenary as the discussion focused on who was and was not Black.

There were differences that had been running through the Black feminist movement and the Black movement in general. There were always rumblings, differences between communities that have never been talked about. These problems exist now. All that happened at Zami I was that they came to the fore. Aqeela Alam

Two groups emerged in 1985-86 which attempted to build community bridges. The Greater London Council provided a small grant for research into the experiences of lesbians from immigrant communities, later to be called the 'Lesbians from Historically Immigrant Communities' (LHIC) project. The interviewees included lesbians of South East Asian, Latin American and Arab descent and the research highlighted the importance of immigration advice from a lesbian perspective. When these issues were raised with interested gay men, it became clear that a lesbian and gay perspective was also needed. Thus the Lesbian and Gay Immigration Group was formed. For five years it provided support and advice and campaigned to raise awareness in the heterosexual and lesbian and gay communities.

In 1985 the Gay Black Group was granted funding by the Greater London Council to establish a centre for Black lesbians and gay men. The group divided its energies between the Black Lesbian and Gay Centre project (BLGC) and the Lesbian and Gay Black Group. BLGC employed workers and throughout the 1980s searched unsuccessfully for accessible and affordable premises in London. In the meantime, the project provided advice, counselling and information to individual Black lesbians and gay men. BLGC also provided training in equal opportunities issues and attempted to increase the visibility of Black lesbians and gay men by liaising with the media. In 1991 BLGC established a one-night-a-week helpline, housed by the Lesbian and Gay Switchboard. In 1992, the project moved to a centre space in south London.

Both the LHIC research and BLGC contributed to discussions to create a broader and clearer definition of Black. BLGC tried to make the term as inclusive of previously unrecognised Black lesbians and gays as possible, including those from Latin America, South East Asia and the Middle East.

Word out

As individuals and members of various groups, Black lesbians contributed to and initiated a number of newsletters, papers and books. Members of OWAAD produced the *FOWAAD* newsletter, the We Are Here conference led to the establishment of a newsletter of the same name, and over the years there were many others. Sadly, most have disappeared without trace.

Outwrite Women's Newspaper, an anti-racist, anti-imperialist monthly, began in 1982 with a collective made up predominantly of Black women, including lesbians. For seven years it reported and commented on women's issues and actions throughout the world. Initially sensitive about its lesbian make-up, *Outwrite* later gained confidence and reported on lesbians in Third World countries as well as in Britain.

The fact that we were all from different countries and coming from different experiences gave it a very exclusive Third World, Black perspective that no other publication had. Teresa Hope

Outwrite grew from a desire to breach the insularity of White feminism and to give voice to Black feminist perspectives. It attempted to interact with the women's movement by debating previously ignored issues and held readers' meetings in different parts of the country as a way of maintaining a broad-based outlook. But by December 1988 the women's movement had broken up and this, coupled with the burn-out suffered by members of the collective and dwindling financial resources, led to the closure of the paper in 1989.

Spare Rib, the monthly national women's liberation magazine, now defunct, was at that time attempting to open its collective and perspective to include Black women and the issues that affected them. *Outwrite's* strength was that it considered Black women and international issues as essential components from the start.

Black Women Talk, a publishing co-operative formed in 1983, is still active in promoting Black women creative writers and is one of the few publishers consistently to include lesbian writers. Sheba Feminist Publishers has regularly published books by Black lesbian writers and included them in anthologies. While many of these have been from the US, Sheba has also published the work of British-based authors Barbara Burford and Jackie Kay. *Charting the Journey: Writings by Black and Third World Women*, published by Sheba in 1988, was the first book to attempt to capture the experiences of Black women in Britain of African, African-Caribbean, Asian and Latin American descent. It included fiction and non-fiction, poetry and prose, lesbians and heterosexual women. The book remains unique in its attempt to represent a wide range of Black women's experiences in this country.

Whose authority?

In the 1980s, some of the large Labour local authorities began to challenge discrimination in their services and employment practices. These initiatives arose primarily as a result of external pressure from local communities and trades unions rather than from the authorities themselves.

Around 1983, after much local lobbying, the London Borough of Islington established a Gay and Lesbian Working Party. Its research showed that though such groups could come up with progressive ideas, unless council staff understood their role in implementing these and/or employees were appointed whose responsibility it was to ensure things happened, nothing would change. Thus the idea of lesbian and gay units surfaced. Working parties with similar aims were also being established within the Greater London Council.

Haringey, another London borough which housed a number of diverse Black communities, set up a Lesbian and Gay Sub-Committee and the first Lesbian and Gay Unit in 1986. The unit employed a number of lesbian and gay workers including at least one Black lesbian. The establishment of the unit was the culmination of nearly two years' hard work by a well-organised local lesbian and gay community, a lesbian and gay group in one of the council's staff unions, Out gay or sympathetic councillors, Labour Party activists and sympathetic senior council officers. Black people were integral to this work and the previous year a lesbian and gay Black and ethnic minority consultative meeting was held to discuss representation on the new sub-committee.

Many Black lesbians remained sceptical about working with or within local government. They believed there were few gains for too much work and that units and their workers were merely tokenistic gestures towards equality. Others felt that over the years Black lesbians would benefit from such units through the organisation of special events, funding of groups and inclusion in council policies.

My view is that we have a right to local authority services. One way or another some of us have to interact with them as tenants, parents, carers, students, but the question is how much faith we place in local authorities. The answer that seems to have emerged is don't trust them. Work through them, but don't put all your energy into them.
Savitri Hensman

Haringey education department set up a working party to look at discrimination against lesbians and gays. Its report outlined the need to encourage an atmosphere of openness in schools, showing children that there was nothing wrong with being lesbian or gay and that some children had lesbian or gay parents. In short, positive images of lesbians and gay men were to be encouraged.

Earlier the local press had got hold of a letter from a worker at the Lesbian and Gay Unit offering to assist head teachers in furthering lesbian and gay equality. The whole issue became grossly distorted and in no time the Parents' Rights Group emerged to capitalise on the publicity. Local Black communities were divided. Some conservative Black community leaders formed a loose alliance with extreme right-wingers, the Parents' Rights Group and the Unification Church.

Haringey Black Action (HBA) was formed to combat these views. It combined Black lesbians and gays and sympathetic heterosexuals in a group which attempted to link the oppressions of race and sexuality. In 1987, along with Positive Images campaigners, HBA organised a national demonstration, Smash the Backlash, which was attended by 4,000 people including many Black lesbians and gay men.

Soon afterwards the Haringey Positive Images policy was agreed. But by the end of the 1980s Clause 28, later Section 2A of the Local Government Act of 1988 forbidding the promotion of homosexuality by local authorities, had been passed by Parliament and many lesbian and gay, women's, disability and race units were being dismantled. It was official – equalities issues were out.

Here and now

Zami II, the second national Black lesbian conference, took place in Birmingham in 1989. Preliminary meetings were held in different cities to ensure that women from all over the country were involved in the conference's planning. The organisers tried to prevent the discussion of who was or was not Black by working to the more inclusive definition used by BLGC, namely those:

descended (through one or both parents) from Africa, Asia (i.e. the Middle East to China, including the Pacific nations) and Latin America, and lesbians and gay men descended from the original inhabitants of Australasia, North America, and the islands of the Atlantic and India Ocean.

Some 200 women attended workshops on sex and sexuality, motherhood, light-skinned/mixed-race lesbians, singing and massage. After the light-skinned/mixed-race workshop, lesbians who had attended initiated a group which met for a number of years, culminating in the formation of MOSAIC, a group for lesbians and gays of mixed racial heritage. At the Zami II plenary, half-aired issues of violence and humiliation among women meant that many lesbians left feeling disillusioned and disappointed.

In the 1990s racism in Britain has increased, alongside homelessness, unemployment, cuts in local authority services, homophobia and repressive immigration measures. The impact on Black lesbians has been profound.

The plethora of Black lesbian groups in London has dwindled to a handful, though groups have emerged in major cities such as Nottingham, Bristol, Birmingham and Manchester. And there are a greater number of Black lesbian and gay groups, although these are attended mainly by men. There has also been a growth in groups organised along lines of ethnicity or national identity. Initially set up as the first step to building alliances, these have now become an end in themselves.

Alongside personal networks, many Black lesbians rely on the lesbian and gay scene, Blues parties and literary or other special events to maintain contact. In the 1980s there was the potential to create a community of, and for, Black lesbians. At the beginning of the 1990s, some feel that the fragmented networks that exist do not constitute such a community.

Out and about

> *Myth. Homosexuality is a White, male, upper and middle class, able-bodied phenomenon found in Europe and North America. When it is found anywhere else it is a result of colonisation. Response. Much of the history of women, Black people, working class people, people with disabilities and people from Africa, Asia and South America has been lost – but where it exists there are many examples of same sex relationships.*
> RISC, 'Human Rights For All?', Reading, 1992, p.74

> *There are, always have been, and always will be lesbians in India and in fact we have quite a long and rich history and tradition of lesbianism and homosexuality.*
> Radio interview aired on WBAI, New York City, 29 April 1984

> *In Nigeria marrying women is old. It is bush ways.* Femi Otitoju

> *Where I come from we use the term wicka. It means women who love women.* Marie

More and more evidence that lesbian relationships existed and were sometimes an accepted part of daily life in our countries of origin is being uncovered. Both positive and negative documentation of lesbian experiences confirms that Black women were practising lesbian behaviour from the beginning of recorded history. In the same countries where homosexual relationships are today a crime, poets and other writers were speaking with affection about same-sex relationships during the Middle Ages and in earlier times. And certainly sexuality in Africa, Asia, the Americas and the Caribbean was expressed more freely before these areas were colonised by Europeans. In some countries, lesbians and gay men were even revered and homosexuality was regarded as a special and precious attribute. These are some of the examples we have come across, from a variety of sources.

In south-west Kenya and north-west Tanzania there are tribes called Kuriar. In the Kuriar tradition, marriage between two women is a legal and accepted ceremony which has been practised for centuries. A wife who is unable to conceive children, especially boys, can marry a surrogate mother.

The mother chooses the man she wants to father her child, but then brings up that child with her wife. It is unusual for the child to know who its father is. Some of these marriages are clearly lesbian arrangements.

Today it has become acceptable for a wealthy Kuriar woman to take a wife rather than live with a man, regardless of whether or not she can have children. This form of marriage can also be found in Nigeria among the Yoruba, Akoko, Nupe and Gana Gana tribes, and in other parts of Africa.

Lesbian bonding by African women does herstorically exist. Lesbian relationships are recognised as legitimate social relationships in certain African Societies.
Vickie M. Mays, 'I hear voices but see no faces. Reflections on racism and woman-identified relationships of Afro-American women', US, 1981

It is known that communities of women into which men were not allowed existed in India. As far back as the fourth century BC it is recorded that autonomous societies made up exclusively of women and known as Stirajya were set up in various parts of India. During the seventh century, Chinese pilgrim Hieun Tsang also makes references to societies of women ruled by female monarchs in China.

If you look at early Hindu scripture and culture you will find a lot of homosexuality suppressed by British culture. Linda Bellos

In the Middle East there was a system of harems in which groups of women – often wives belonging to one husband – lived together and reared children. Harem meant 'keep out', and it was considered a great privilege for men to be invited in to watch the women dance and entertain. Some women had intimate relationships with each other that were celebrated among themselves and reputed to involve lesbian behaviour. Writers from 500AD describe harems as 'hot-beds' of lesbianism.

Evidence of the existence of lesbian relationships in these countries in more recent times has occasionally crept into the media. For example in November 1979, a daily Indian newspaper reported a case of two girls in Ahmedabad who ended their lives by jumping in front of a train. They had been forced to enter arranged marriages the previous year and found themselves unable to live apart. In 1981 an Indonesian magazine reported what it believed to be the first lesbian couple in Indonesia. The women held a ceremony to celebrate their union and were congratulated by over 100 guests, including their families.

The late Audre Lorde, in her book *Zami*, describes how women in Carriacou would move their lesbian lovers into their homes when their husbands went away for work. When the men returned some women would continue their same-sex relationships as before, while others would allow their husbands to move back in but would conduct their relationships with women outside the marital home. These women are described as 'making zami'. In Surinam they are called Mati, Mati.

In Carriacou lesbianism is seen as a phase you go through. I made love
to so many women on the island, they threw me off. Madge

Today lesbianism is not accepted in many of the countries from which we
originate. Some women cohabit with men and meet their female lovers in
secret. Others have fled their countries out of fear of persecution, leaving
behind families and children. For others, it is an issue of life and death.

In Pakistan, homosexual sex by men or women is a crime punished by
100 lashes, which sometimes results in death. It is also a crime in Iran, where
a lesbian or gay man who is caught can sometimes be sentenced to death.
There is also unofficial, systematic persecution of homosexuals in Colombia,
while Trinidad has ruled homosexuality illegal.

But Britain is not necessarily a safe haven for Black lesbians who leave
their countries to escape oppressive regimes, extreme harassment or laws
against their sexuality. Constant immigration checks by police and home-
office officials mean that many Black lesbians in Britain continue to live in fear.

The White disease

Lesbianism is known in many of the different Black communities as the White
disease. The implication is that the arrival of homosexuality in our
communities is the fault of White people and of colonisation. The notion of
homosexuality as a White disease is reinforced by the absence of visible Black
lesbians and gay men. Most media representations of lesbians and gays are
of White people and fewer Black people are prepared to be Out.

Because Black communities already experience discrimination on
grounds of race, colour and language, there is a fear among the heterosexual
population that to admit to the existence of a taboo like homosexuality
would oppress them even more, dragging them further into the gutter. It is
almost as though we have let the side down by being lesbian or gay. To call
homosexuality a White disease is like saying, 'we don't want to discuss this,
we don't want to deal with it, it has nothing to do with us.'

**Often they say that only White women can be lesbians and feminists,
because there's something wrong with them. Marlene Bogle**

*Many Black people think that Black lesbians and gay men have been
corrupted by White lesbians and gays... and so have left their roots behind.*
NALGO, 'Lesbian and Gays Organising Together', London, NALGO Press,
1991, p.40

It is as though much of the Black heterosexual population conveniently
chooses to believe that lesbians do not exist in Africa, Asia, the Caribbean,
the Americas and other Black indigenous cultures. But the existence of
lesbians in our countries of origin is a fact. The difference is that whereas in
Africa, Asia and the Caribbean it is common practice for lesbians to remain
in a heterosexual unit and have lesbian relationships outside the marital

home, in Britain Black lesbians are more likely to leave their communities to live with their female lovers. Others may compromise by marrying and living with a gay man from their country of origin so they can continue their lesbian relationships without pressure to marry from their families. Perhaps when the Black heterosexual population denies the existence of Black lesbians, what they are saying is: 'we don't have women "back home" who live like lesbians in Britain.'

I try telling my community that lesbianism has been going on for a long time. While the men are out working, the women are enjoying themselves bad. I've seen it myself. Marlene Bogle

I'm often told that I'm a lesbian because I was brought up in England. My reply is, it is because I was brought up in England that I choose to live with a woman and tell people about it. If I was brought up in Nigeria, I would just be having sex with women and not telling anyone. Femi Otitoju

Homophobia

Saying that homophobia is more prevalent in the Black community is like saying there are more Black men who rape. Linda Bellos

It is a dirty, vicious lie that the Black community is more homophobic. This is racism. Go to any community with a strong religion or faith, and see how homophobic they are. Femi Otitoju

It is a racist myth that Black communities are more homophobic than White communities. First, this belief suggests that the many different Black populations in Britain are one homogeneous group with the same religious, cultural, class and social backgrounds. Second, homophobia is prevalent in most societies today, where heterosexuality is perceived as the norm and anything different as perverse, a type of mental illness that needs to be cured.

Religion is fundamental to many Black people living in Britain. Christianity, Hinduism, Islam and other beliefs such as Rastafarianism have been important to maintain a sense of community in the face of racism. So because Black communities seem to cling on to their religious or cultural traditions – many of which are riddled with homophobic contempt – it may appear on the surface that they are more homophobic than White people. In addition, fewer Black people are visible in the mainstream, which makes it more noticeable when homophobic comments are made by Black people in the media, popular culture and at political events.

My family are Seventh Day Adventists, so I have sinned. It is a sin to be a lesbian. Hope Massiah

Many Black lesbians desire solidarity with their Black peers and families, and wish to maintain strong links with their communities. Black lesbians feel the pain more strongly when people from their own communities attack them.

I've had more aggravation from Black men, not to mention physical assault, than from any other section of the population living in Britain. And it hurts. B: England P: US/England (QR)

If the Black communities in Britain demand a society of equal rights and opportunities, an end to racism and discrimination, then it is imperative that they respect the rights of other oppressed groups such as lesbians and gay men. Black lesbians contribute to our communities as mothers, carers, doctors, lawyers, community workers, politicians, teachers, actors, writers, tradeswomen, manual workers and so on: the view that lesbians threaten the future of the Black family and race is a ridiculous myth. But unfortunately some sections of the Black communities in Britain have demonstrated attitudes to their lesbian and gay populations as narrow-minded as those associated with racist bigotry.

The case of 'The Voice'

Every society has its watchdogs, and Black communities too have their politicians, community leaders, media outlets, public figures and institutions whom the population looks to for guidance. When a high-profile person or establishment supports homophobic abuse, it divides and weakens whole communities.

In 1990, Britain's widely read Black national newspaper *The Voice*, which caters predominantly to the African and Caribbean communities, behaved in as bigoted a way as the racist, sexist and homophobic national daily, *The Sun*. *The Voice* carried headlines that read, 'Why Gays aren't fit to be Parents' and 'I'm no Lesbo, says Whitney'. Then in the week of 30 October, it ran four pages of news and editorial attacking the professional Black footballer Justin Fashunu for Coming Out as gay. In the same issue, the Nigerian High Commission in London was quoted as saying: 'In Nigeria we treat homosexuals with utter contempt. Gay children are often disowned.' And *The Voice* columnist Tony Sewell wrote: 'Homosexuals are the greatest queer bashers around. No other group are so preoccupied with making their own sexuality look dirty.'

In response, members of the Black lesbian and gay community formed Black Lesbians And Gays Against Media Homophobia (BLAGAMH), which initiated an effective campaign to boycott the paper. The group won the support of the National Association of Local Government Officers (NALGO), which instructed all its members to back the campaign and persuaded several local authorities to ban advertising in *The Voice*.

In September 1991 the boycott was lifted, after *The Voice* had agreed to give BLAGAMH a one-page right of reply, made a commitment to positive reporting on lesbian and gay issues, and agreed to implement an equal opportunities policy for the newspaper's employees. A year later publisher Val McCalla said:

The issue of homosexuality is entirely new to the West Indian community, who are extremely conservative. The Voice is not homophobic.
Radio Four, 'Worktalk', 9 October 1992

Since then BLAGAMH has challenged reggae artists such as Buju Banton, whose lyrics state that lesbians and gays should be shot, and Shabba Ranks, who claimed that homosexuals 'deserve crucifixion'. Yet these artists are merely the tip of the iceberg and homophobic incitement by some Black singers, rappers and toasters is virulent. Many Black youth party all night to music that promotes homophobia, misogyny and sexism.

Homophobia is one of the few issues that can unite White racists and Black communities, as demonstrated by the debate over Haringey Council's introduction of a Positive Images policy into schools in 1987 in an attempt to encourage a spirit of openness about lesbian and gay lifestyles.

At council meetings where the issue of Positive Images came up... there were extreme right-wingers hurling racist abuse at councillors. At the same time next to them were Black people aligned with them against Positive Images. Savitri Hensman

Coming Out

More and more Black lesbians today can be open about their sexuality. But to Come Out as a lesbian in a Black community can still be traumatic. And some communities still disown their lesbian daughters. Many Black women see their communities as a safe space in which they are protected from the institutionalised and individual racism they experience in Britain. So for many Black lesbians, the support of their communities is of great importance.

Like all lesbians, there are some of us who choose to be Out in every aspect of our lives and others who are Out only to friends. How Out we decide to be is always an individual choice, influenced by our work, family and cultural background. Since Coming Out can mean loss of family, friends, cultural bereavement, isolation, nervous breakdown, forced arranged marriage or fear for our lives, it is hardly surprising that some lesbians choose to lead a double life rather than lose the support and safety of their communities. To leave behind family, friends and a cultural identity for the sake of being Out can be a high price to pay.

If my family gets to know I'm a lesbian, unless I become a millionaire, they might kill me because my life has no value.
B: Middle East P: Middle East (LHIC)

I've had cases of young Asian lesbians, aged 17 and 18, attempting to commit suicide in order to escape from home and arranged marriages, and they've ended up in mental hospitals. Teresa Hope

I don't think I'd ever be able to Come Out publicly – my family in Turkey feels that if I Came Out any further, they would have to Come Out too. They feel I have no right to impose that on them. Zehra

My mother went apeshit, and behaved the way Nigerian parents do. She called every single aunt and uncle I had, and begged them to talk to me for God's sake, and the sake of their lives. Femi Otitoju

The first person I let know was my mother. I told her I was a lesbian, and that I was sexually abused by my father, at the same time. Her initial reaction was shock, horror and revulsion. She blanked it all out for five years as though I had never told her. Marlene Bogle

I have Come Out to all sorts of people within my own community. One 60-year-old religious Asian woman, on finding out, said: 'But daughter, I only got married because I had to.' And yet, I've also experienced the most unexpected hostility from young trendy Asians. Aqeela Alam

For others Coming Out is an empowering experience – relief, the breaking of silence, the arrival of sanity. When Black lesbians first Come Out they often believe they are the only ones. They enter a new environment dominated by White women, which promotes a White culture entrenched in racism.

I used to think that if I said I was a lesbian it would mean I had to sleep with White women, because whenever I saw a Black lesbian out she was always with a White lesbian. It was a relief to find Black lesbians with other Black women. Dorothea Smartt

The organisation of Black lesbian groups, conferences and women-only parties and the creation of images and writings by and about Black lesbians have played an important role in validating our experience. Attending a Black lesbian-only event for the first time can be similar to Coming Out all over again: relief, excitement and nervousness accompanying the discovery of other Black lesbians with similar backgrounds.

It was fucking tough for Black women to Come Out as lesbians in Brighton. You were basically meat, or exotic. Within months of Coming Out I moved to London, where I found other Black women who were as angry as I was. Linda Bellos

I Came Out aged 23. It was traumatic because for six months I felt like I was carrying my sexuality around my neck. I decided that if I was going to be a lesbian, I needed to meet other Black lesbians. So I went to Peckham Black Lesbian Group. Hope Massiah

I walked through the door of a party, and the walls were lined with Black women, squeezed up in compromising positions in a half-dark room. This is what I had been looking for. I felt an enormous sense of satisfaction and relief. Dorothea Smartt

Separate worlds

The segregation of the sexes has been practised in non-western cultures for centuries. In Australia the indigenous inhabitants have women's business and men's business – sacred sites on to which members of the opposite sex are not allowed as well as subjects which are talked about only among members of the same sex and traditions specific to each gender. In Africa and India there are communities of women who live together with their children, practising their own rituals, dances and ceremonies. In some non-western and non-Christian societies, same-sex communities are the norm.

Black separatism arose as a political position during the Civil Rights movement of the 1950s and 60s in the US. Some African-American activists thought that groups campaigning against segregation should be made up only of them; others argued that to work with White people against White laws would give the movement more power. In the 1960s it was accepted that the Black Power movement would adopt Black separatism as its model.

During the late 1960s and 70s some feminists adopted separatism as a political strategy and way of life. Women believed that because men dominated every aspect of their lives, spaces free of them were essential to enable women to organise and execute the fight against male power. The existence of separatist communities has been of great value to women who have needed places free from male violence, sexism and misogyny. But to sever all links with men has not necessarily been a sensible or satisfactory strategy for Black women, who have needed to join ranks with Black men to fight racism and oppression.

Lesbian separatism

For some lesbians separatism is a political position; for others it is about self-healing, placing energy in other women and creating safe spaces in a hostile world. Both heterosexuals and gay men find it difficult to understand that separatist spaces are important for female and lesbian personal growth, with the result that lesbians who will not mix with men have been accused of being man-haters. Many Black lesbians find the concept of lesbian separatism too restrictive, since racism is still an issue in the largely White lesbian community, and this can be just as oppressive as sexism or homophobia. Some Black lesbians believe that separatism of any kind is an impossible option because the oppressions they experience take many forms and require a range of actions and alliances to combat them.

When faced with what could seem like a choice between White women and Black men, some Black lesbians choose to align themselves with Black men because race is a more important issue to them than sexuality.

Although my sexuality is an integral part of myself, race is in general more significant. If I had to choose between two groups of people, one of mainly White dykes and the other of Black men, nine times out of ten I would choose the latter. Linda Bellos

I have more in common with a Black man because he experiences racism and some forms of discrimination like I do. White lesbians would not have an idea about the racism I experience... I disagree with lesbian separatists because I don't feel I could live in a cocoon... I would be excluding people I love and care for. I have young male children in my family. I would like to feel that I have some input into making them better men. Marlene Bogle

But there are many Black lesbians who see lesbian separatism as valuable and incorporate aspects of it into their lifestyles. It seems that when we first Come Out, many of us pass through a period of lesbian separatism which is almost always empowering and strengthening. But few of those interviewed felt they wanted this to be a fixed position.

I believe in working entirely for women. I believe in autonomy... A period of separatism can be very healing, and allow personal growth... I would never live permanently as a separatist because I don't think women will ever be able to snatch the power. Femi Otitoju

Separatism was a necessary phase I went through, it helped me get my head together and move away from home. Finding myself with other women made me strong enough to go back into the world. I respect separatism as a phase but not as an end in itself. Linda Bellos

I feel that in order to survive as a lesbian, you need a lesbian environment... There are a number of things I wouldn't debate with heterosexuals, however lovely they might be. It is a necessary step for lesbians to be separatist in this very hateful world. It's vital that you spend time and energy on your own kind. Teresa Hope

In my heart of hearts I'm a separatist. It's about where and how you place your energies when given the choice. It's not about building a house in Wales and not having any male sheep on it. Anne Hayfield

Black lesbian separatism

Black lesbian separatists are women who have relationships only with Black lesbians and live and work with them wherever possible. Some Black lesbian separatists see this as an invaluable political strategy and permanent way of life; others believe it is an essential stage all Black lesbians should experience. Some separatists continue to communicate with their male relatives; others have nothing to do with them.

Black lesbian separatism should be recommended for all Black lesbians at some stage. Being with people like you for a while gives you room to find out who you are. It's important to get away from racism and heterosexism. Separatism is about personal growth, strength, common identity and support. Femi Otitoju

I think as a gathering strategy it can be very efficient to find people with common denominators; it's the first thing you do to organise politically, but it's only the first stage. I would insist that some things are for Latin American lesbians only. Teresa Hope

Your chances of being able to become a whole person are more if you're not relating to White people at close quarters. Aqeela Alam

While most Black lesbians enjoy and value some forms of Black lesbian separatism – support groups, conferences or social events – it is not a lifestyle or ideology with which all Black lesbians feel at home.

I don't subscribe to Black lesbian separatism because I would like to have a much wider view of the world. There is a time and a place for Black lesbians to get together without White women around, and there are times when Black and White lesbians should get together to discuss certain things. Araba Mercer

Black lesbian separatism is not for me because there are White women I care about, and have as friends. Hope Massiah

Relationships between Black women

Sexual, platonic and working relationships between Black women are free of the racism with which White women can oppress us. But as Black lesbians from different backgrounds, we have prejudices that can oppress other Black women. Black lesbians in Britain find themselves within a system which places our races in a hierarchy. For example, African-Caribbeans are seen as illiterate, aggressive, troublesome; South and South East Asians as intelligent, passive and submissive. At times we have colluded with this.

There has been little dialogue about the prejudices we bring from our wider communities, and despite our common experiences, organising, socialising and discussion can at times be difficult and painful.

I enjoy working and having personal relationships with other Black women. But we all walk with our baggage. Still, we have a shared common ground to begin from and I'm more willing to put my energy

into relationships with all the different kinds of Black women, so I can understand Black women from different cultures. Dorothea Smartt

Same-race relationships are free of racism. However, they can be more difficult because you are a reflection of each other... When push comes to shove you can't scream: 'Oh, you're just a racist.' However, they are really wonderful and spiritual. You don't have to explain things all the time. Hope Massiah

I have to admit I may never know what it's like to be Indian, Chinese or Pakistani, but we have common ground. Having relationships with other Black women from different cultures is a learning and growing thing. Araba Mercer

With another Black woman we can share the pain of racism and we don't have to explain. The fact that I'm a Black Jew and my lover is a Hindu I find strengthening. Different experiences can make a relationship richer. Linda Bellos

Relationships with White women

Since the meetings of the first Black lesbian group in the early 1980s, whether or not Black lesbians should have relationships with White women has been a volatile subject. Some Black lesbians have argued that once they had found other Black lesbians, there was no need to have relationships with White women.

A big issue was to sleep or not to sleep with White women. This was like a little time bomb. Dorothea Smartt

I stopped attending Black lesbian group meetings because I went from being one of the corner-pins to being marginal. I was ostracised for leaving a Black lover and having a relationship with a White woman. I was told I had let the side down and was accused of selling out. Femi Otitoju

Sexual, platonic and working relationships with White women are still frowned upon by some Black lesbians. Black lesbians who have intimate relationships with White women are accused of selling out on their culture or are considered confused and out of touch with their identities. What this attitude ignores is that relationships can be healthy or unhealthy whether they are with Black or White women. It also denies the experience of Black lesbians who have grown up in intimate relationships with White people, a White parent, White adoptive foster parents or in children's homes.

And some Black lesbians live in areas where few Black lesbians are Out, making relationships with other Black women almost impossible.

I mix with White women a lot, it was either that or go back in the closet. I started going to the Older Lesbian Network after my relationship broke up and I really needed it. That's why I will not knock stuff that White

people give, because they were there when I needed it, and I'm still friends with some of those women now. Marie

Relationships with White women can be healthy, but there can be problems around language, culture, expression and space. Araba Mercer

I don't think making love to a White woman is any different from making love to a Black woman. All my life in this country I've had four beautiful relationships. Three were with White women and the fourth was with a Black woman. Madge

I thought I would never have a relationship with a White woman but I did. Although it didn't work out we did have some common ground. Marlene Bogle

But even in otherwise healthy relationships between Black and White women, racism is always on the agenda. For some Black lesbians it has made relationships with White women impossible to contemplate.

There was a period when I would not have a relationship with a White woman because of racism. The pain of having to explain hurt and deal with racism was too much. I didn't want to, I didn't need to, I couldn't cope, I did not want to engage with White women. Linda Bellos

Relationships with White women are fraught with difficulties. I've been in relationships with White women, and although they were good, the issue of racism was always there. You cannot escape from racism. Hope Massiah

In general relationships with White women are fine. In reality I see a tremendous amount of abuse – abuse of power and lack of respect from White women. Femi Otitoju

Today my expectations of White lesbians are more realistic. Relationships can work if both women are in a space which allows it. Dorothea Smartt

The only White lesbians I have as friends are people I've known for a long time. I'm not really open to making friendships with White lesbians any more. I'm not really into having relationships with White women either. Anne Hayfield

Relationships with men

Black lesbians and gay men have worked together to create successful organisations, support and pressure groups, as in the work of the Black Lesbian and Gay Centre in London and several smaller groups around Britain. But such collaborations do produce problems, and women involved often feel subject to sexism, misogyny and lack of understanding. Black women's issues are not usually a priority on men's agendas – most are unaware of or ignore the fact that they too contribute to our oppression. Too often when we work together the men are the public spokespeople while the women rally round as secretaries doing most of the hard work.

Black gay men need to deal with issues of sexism before we can work productively together. Dorothea Smartt

Relationships between Black lesbians and gay men seem fraught with tension because of desperately wanting and needing each other. There is something inherent in our different lifestyles which means we can only work well together for a limited amount of time. Black gay men are not politically thought out. Araba Mercer

They don't know what a woman is. I assumed that there would be a little more effort and care among Black gay men who profess political awareness, who profess some interest in truth, spirit and justice, to grasp the idea of what a woman is, rather than assume she's a gay male without a dick. Anna Juleya Hearne

Black lesbians rarely attended the Black Lesbian and Gay Group meetings in London during the 1980s because they felt uncomfortable. Black gay men's experiences are entirely different from ours. Femi Otitoju

On a personal level, some of us have managed to establish good friendships with Black gay men. For women who live in areas where there are few visible Black lesbians, links with Black gay men can be very important. There are also positive aspects to mixing with Black gay men as ways of strengthening our identity and challenging homophobia in our communities.

White men

I think White gay men as a whole are a pain in the arse. Their political awareness about women's issues and women's oppression is lacking. They feel persecuted by the rest of society and so they have developed their own microcosm in which they hate everyone else. So racism and misogyny are just endemic within that community. Anne Hayfield

Successful working relationships with White gay men are less common. Organisations which cater for lesbians and gays are usually dominated by White men, along with a few White women. Most of the women interviewed had little to say about relationships with White men.

However, friendships and work relationships do exist and some are productive and healthy. Separatism is only part of the way we as Black lesbians explore our identities.

Black: whose term is it anyway?

In the days of slavery and forced transportation of people around the world, terms such as coloured, brown, red or Black were used by colonisers to describe Africans, Chinese, Native Americans and Australians, Indians and those from the Middle East – in fact anyone who was not classed as White. Gradually Black grew to be a term of abuse. It was reclaimed in the US of the 1960s by the Black Power movement, which drew on the legacy of early twentieth-century African-American writers in using Black as a key element in forging a positive identity and conveying a sense of racial pride.

The importance of this essentially African-American politics to Britain did not initially create a mono-racial view of Black peoples. Black was used at times to mean people of African descent and at others as an umbrella term inclusive of other groups. For example, the National Black Peoples' Alliance (NBPA) was set up in 1962 as a 'militant front for Black consciousness and against racialism'. NBPA was made up of representatives from the National Federation of Pakistani Associations, Universal Coloured Peoples Association, West Indian Standing Conference and Indian Workers Associations. Groups such as NBPA were also inspired by the increasing recognition of a common oppression among those struggling against colonialism and imperialism in Africa, Asia and Latin America. But the mainstream media cared little for our distinctions: we were all foreigners, immigrants, Blacks or coloureds.

By the time Black lesbians began organising in Britain, few remembered that Black as an identity was historically and geographically specific. By then it was easy for British-based Black people, including lesbians, to vent years of frustration, pain and anger indiscriminately on White people, who were regarded as the sole or primary source of our oppression.

In the course of trying to build a strong sense of British Blackness, reality was over-simplified and several damaging myths were spawned.
- In a world divided into Black and White it is essential to know who is who.
- Black is an internationally recognised and used term for our identity.
- Black people grow up identifying as such.
- If you come to identify as Black later in life, you have probably been 'passing' yourself off as White or White-identified, and so do not qualify as Black.
- The term Black implies African-Caribbean.

Among Black lesbians numerous opportunities for working on issues crucial to our survival were lost while we painfully and pointlessly debated who was and was not Black.

I don't believe the Black lesbian movement has dealt with the issues of White racism, intra-racism, or internalised racism, right down to the fact that no one will use the term intra-racism. That denial is based on a lack of confidence, always wanting Whites to be the ones in authority. In a world where inter-racial hatred between people of common origin is at such a pitch, it's a privilege for Black people here to maintain that the only hostility, the only issue to be addressed is White people's racism. Anna Juleya Hearne

When you separate the world up into Black and White, it feels like the world is half Black and half White. This makes White people far too important, because they make up only a tiny part of the world. Hope Massiah

In order to claim a Black identity and in the name of unity we simplified our complex racial herstories and routes to this country. We condensed our experiences until they met the requirements of the myths and felt ashamed and/or defensive if they did not. The alternative was to float in an identity limbo, because there was no fixed place for some of us in a community that saw things only in terms of Black or White. And yet few of us lived up to the myths of a British-based Black identity.

Black is a very British term and if you've just come from India, nobody tells you at the airport you're now supposed to call yourself Black. To me that is part of the British colonialist culture that has seeped into Black people born in this country. Aqeela Alam

The first time I realised I was Black was when I came to England. In Jamaica being Black wasn't an issue. Marlene Bogle

I am Black in my existence here in England, but personally I'm Latin American, which is different, in the same way that African or Caribbean is different. Teresa Hope

Because I don't have a dark skin colour I feel that I'm considered White and shouldn't be at Black lesbian events. B: England P: Cyprus (QR)

I'm probably not 'Black enough' for many people, I don't like reggae and I don't understand patois. B: UK P: Nigeria (QR)

The assumptions of British Black identity left no space for Black lesbians born overseas to articulate their experiences of being dislocated, uprooted, belonging nowhere. Neither was there much care or concern for the physical and psychological toll exacted.

The most racist face of the British state is its immigration controls, and it exercises these in a very thorough way. For instance, it stops you

bringing your kids in for three years, but by then they've missed a crucial part of their education... Everywhere you are there are extensions of those controls. Everything centres around the fact that you don't belong here – so what the hell are you doing here? Zehra

Without a doubt I wouldn't be who I am today if I hadn't lived here all these years. But I've paid a price for it. The person who relates to the world isn't the whole me. Some integral part of myself, of my cultural heritage has atrophied, because it was the only way I knew to survive. Da Choong

It takes me much longer to explain something than it would native English speakers and most people are unwilling to wait until I finish. They're too impatient and that takes its toll. You either shut up or you talk on and people ignore you. Zehra

Nor did the Black lesbian community provide a place for those born overseas to talk of how invisible, isolated and silenced they felt within British society, including among Black lesbians.

It's that Blacker-than-thou mentality you have to face, that's the reality a Woman of Colour, born overseas, experiences here. There's neither interest, nor respect, it's yet another part of my identity I'm meant to silence or forget. Anna Juleya Hearne

I think there are similarities in the way I've experienced myself within the predominantly White lesbian community I Came Out in and the Black lesbian community I came to later. There is some degree of adjustment I'm supposed to make either way. It's been hard to have open discussions about my feeling that I'm accepted as long as I don't draw attention to my particular experience, which may vastly differ from theirs, or challenge the usefulness of a hierarchy of oppression (and implicit within that, people of African descent being the most oppressed). Da Choong

My political outlook is perhaps different from most British-born Black lesbians... I'm less likely to idealise 'back home'. Savitri Hensman

I find Black lesbians born in this country are very English. They don't think so and that's the tragedy. They lack true warmth and have a shallow sense of pride in their Black identity. B: Trinidad P: Jamaica/Trinidad (QR)

Threat to whose race?

Common to White and Black communities in Britain is the fear of inter-racial relationships. These are viewed as a potential threat to the 'purity' of the race and a betrayal of one's community. The children of these relationships are welcomed by neither community, denied the right to claim their own identity and open to being labelled by all. Adulthood doesn't change this.

I've been called a Black slut, I've been called a White slut, I've been called a half-Black slut, I've been called a half-White slut. I've been used by White male attitudes to fulfil some illusion of what a Black woman is and I've been equally vulnerable to being used by Black male attitudes towards White femaleness. Anna Juleya Hearne

I have been called a half-breed in some Black women's groups.
B: England P: Nigeria/Poland (QR)

As more and more women Came Out as lesbians, there was the hope of creating a forum made up of all Black lesbians in which issues of identity could be addressed. Sadly, the entrenchment of the Black myths left no room for such a discussion. Instead more Black lesbians have been left feeling outsiders within their own community.

I'm not always accepted or acknowledged as Black, I'm seen or assumed to be White, like guilty until proven otherwise.
B: England P: India/England (QR)

I've given up wanting recognition. I'm not White, I'm not Black. I'm mixed race, a nothing – I guess it's a problem not knowing my father's origins... I feel I don't belong anywhere. B: England P: Ireland/Unknown (QR)

As I look 'light' I am not readily accepted by the Black lesbian community. Most people are surprised and suspicious.
B: England P: Ireland/Cuba (QR)

This whole debate, whether inside the Black lesbian community or in the wider society, is essentially flawed. It is usually based on the idea that we are mono-racial in our heritage, through birth, culture and upbringing. For example, it ignores the fact that some of us are brought up by White birth, foster or adoptive parents. It is also ahistorical, based on the false belief that despite 500 years of colonialism and imperialism, forced transportation and wholesale rape of Black women, we in Britain could constitute 'pure' Black races. It ignores the fact that there are Caribbean people of Chinese, Indian, Middle Eastern and European descent; Africans of Chinese or Asian descent; Latin Americans who have European, Native American, Japanese or African ancestors; Cypriots of Arab, African and Indian heritage.

I'm second-generation African, but my grandparents were from the Indian sub-continent, therefore I identify ethnically and culturally as an Asian. B: Tanzania P: Tanzania/Kenya (QR)

I want more acceptance of those of us who don't have a fucking easy cultural identity! I don't belong completely to the Asian or European community and I feel like a little island floating around on my own. Some of us are proud of both and want to acknowledge both. B: England P: India/Germany (QR)

I define myself as Black politically, but recognise my background is very different both from that of my first-generation parents and from that of my Black peers who are often from the Caribbean. My immersion in English culture very definitely helps make up my identity – for good or bad. B: UK P: Nigeria (QR)

[I define myself as] Nigerian British, because both my parents are Nigerian and I have a fair amount of contact with Nigerians. But I was brought up in Britain and I had English foster parents, so inevitably I have taken on a lot of British culture. B: England P: Nigeria (QR)

Our identities have been pared down or silenced in the name of Black unity. There seems little recognition that ideas of racial or ethnic 'purity' are an ineffective and dangerous response to White racism.

But despite the pressure to simplify our complex racial backgrounds, some Black lesbians have persevered in attempting to name our herstories appropriately. The term mixed race, while an improvement on half-caste, is still regarded as an inexact shorthand for being born of one White and one Black parent. Not all of us who are racially 'mixed' conform to this model. The term of mixed racial parentage has possibilities, but still defines us on the basis of the racial background of our parents, ignoring the fact that for some of us the racial 'mix' occurred further back than this. And there are other reasons for dissatisfaction with the term.

I define myself as of mixed racial heritage, rather than of mixed racial parentage, because I'm not my parents. It's one step closer to self-definition. Mixed racial parentage makes me feel like some kind of biological experiment of my parents, which I was, but I don't have to submit to that destiny. I can claim what is for me, over and above what my parents were and are. In a world where adults oppress and abuse children and adultism exists, I think it should be fed as little as possible and mixed racial parentage feeds this. Anna Juleya Hearne

The term mixed racial heritage provides a possible answer. In recent years it has grown in popularity among lesbians and gay men. MOSAIC, a group for lesbians and gays of mixed racial heritage, was formed after a workshop of the same name held at the 1990 International Lesbian and Gay People of Colour conference in London. In 1993 MOSAIC staged its first national meeting. The appeal of the term of mixed racial heritage is that it has more flexibility to include, rather than exclude, our experiences.

Under the umbrella Black

In an attempt to break the tyranny of the unspoken myths regarding Black identity, Black lesbians began to qualify what or who the term Black included each time it was used. But this has not proved satisfactory.

Groups might say 'Black means...' and use some exact definition, but

inevitably when I got to the door, I'd always be checked out. I had to end up giving a potted family history! I never felt relaxed in the knowledge that this would be a safe welcoming space for me.
B: England P: Germany/India (QR)

I think the term means so many different things to different groups that it needs always to define itself further. B: England P: Nigeria (QR)

Black is a colour word, it gives us the sense of one thing and not the sense of people getting together. I would like a term which signifies people of different cultures coming together. Hope Massiah

[Black] doesn't have one definition used and understood by everyone and it doesn't speak of our differences, but lumps us as one, which is like the 'they're all the same' mentality. B: England P: India/England (QR)

Black has loads of different meanings according to who you are and where you're standing at the time. I have felt accepted within the Black lesbian community often on the basis of being acknowledged by women of African descent who are well established within that community. Since I'm accepted by them, others accept me too. But the likelihood of my being challenged at a Black lesbian event/meeting, where no one knows me, is always there, even now. Da Choong

It's clear that Black has not succeeded in being inclusive of us all. Should we try to forge a term that will provide us with an umbrella under which we may all stand a chance of being accepted in all our racial complexity? In common usage in the US is the term Lesbians of Colo(u)r. Could it work for us? In Britain there have been fierce arguments against it – fears that it could be regarded as inclusive of White people or a dislike of it because it is reminiscent of the term coloured. Others believe that Black has more political weight and have fought for so long for it to be an inclusive term that to take on Lesbians of Colour would feel like giving up. However, many lesbians unsure of their inclusion under the term Black feel clearer and more at home with of Colour.

I love the term of Colour. That describes me. Black events are inevitably mainly Afro-Caribbean. B: England P: India/Germany (QR)

I would be quite happy to use another term – one that incorporates that particular political perspective – if there was broad consensus on it. I've always been partial to Women of Colour, which aptly expresses diversity as well as commonality of experience; but there has always been strong objection to that term in this country. Da Choong

Black, with its attendant myths, has been used by us to divide us. Identifying as Lesbians of Colour will not heal the rifts, but at least it might enable us all to be admitted into the same space together.

If the label fits, wear it

❦ The labels you use to describe yourself are important. I think that any labels we have are only there because of the society we live in. I mean, look at the plethora of them.❦ Jackie Kay

Labelling – placing people in rigid categories and imposing a name tag – has been a common feature of colonisation. Often names have been imposed on us from the outside and sometimes Black people have used these labels to help create an identity. For example, by reclaiming as positive words such as Black that were once used to denigrate us.

Dominant White British culture is full of racist language and images. And in the lesbian and gay world, the terminology which has developed is born out of White western experience. Black lesbians live in an environment which presumes that to be White is the norm, so words such as woman or gay, used without the prefix Black or a country of origin, are assumed to refer to White people. Black lesbians need to create their own words that refer to their specific experiences and place them at the centre of the English language. What follows are some of the words we as Black lesbians use to describe ourselves and our opinions about them.

Zami

Zami is a Caribbean word particular to the island of Carriacou. The late Audre Lorde in her book *Zami: A New Spelling of My Name* (1982) uses zami to describe women who have sexual and loving relationships with each other. Since then some Black women have used zami to define their sexual preference and it was the name used for the two Black lesbian conferences, Zami I and II. However, some Black lesbians have not heard of it.

I use zami because it comes out of an African-Caribbean culture. It refers to women loving women and supporting women. It refers to sexual practice as well as to communities of women surviving and doing things together. Zami means one or all of these things. Dorothea Smartt

Zami is a term we use back home. I don't like handles. As far as I'm concerned, I'm a woman loving women. Madge

I use zami when I don't want people generally to understand what I'm talking about. Aqeela Alam

I have a problem with zami because it's what I call Afrekeke. It conjures up the type of Black women who walk around with African prints on, and say if you don't wear ethnic clothes you're not Black enough. Araba Mercer

Zami is about an experience in the Caribbean. The words lesbian or zami do not have to be transferred geographically; each definition describes a particular experience. Femi Otitoju

Khush

Khush is an Urdu word which came originally from Indian culture, where it means gay and happy and also signifies ecstatic pleasure. The term has become popular among some Asian lesbians and gay men. British-based film director Pratibha Parmar named her television documentary about South Asian lesbians and gay men *Khush*.

Khush is not a word that says lesbian or indeed anything else about your sexuality. It means happy, and doesn't even have the same double meaning as gay has. In modern-day Urdu it doesn't mean anything. Khush is correctly pronounced hush, but no one says it properly and that is one of the reasons I don't like using it. Aqeela Alam

Khush and zami are terms from India and Africa, I'm a Sri Lankan lesbian.
B: Sri Lanka P: Sri Lanka/England (QR)

Lesbian

Lesbian is an English word derived from the name for the inhabitants of the Greek island Lesbos, where the woman-loving poet Sappho lived in the sixth century BC. It has been used to describe women whose personal identity and lifestyle are based on emotional and sexual desire for and relationships with other women.

Lesbian implies a predominantly Eurocentric aesthetic about sex and sexuality. Dorothea Smartt

My best definition is Black lesbian because our experiences are totally different from those of White lesbians. Marlene Bogle

I identify with lesbian because I Came Out through the Women's Liberation Movement, where White women supported me in my sexuality. Lesbian identifies me, because it is part of the European culture within which I was brought up, and which allowed me to find an identity. Femi Otitoju

Dyke

Dyke is derived from the American word Bulldike. The origins of Bulldike are not known, though it is likely that the word came from African-American culture since it appears in Blues songs of the 1930s. (Bessie Jackson recorded a song in 1935 called 'B-D Blues' which refers to Bulldike.)

Dyke appears in American slang dictionaries of the 1940s as a word for a woman who adopts masculine, butch roles. It is possible that dyke got its connotations of masculinity through association with African-American culture: during American and British slavery, women of African descent were forced to do traditional male jobs and were rarely perceived as feminine by White people. White lesbians in Britain and the US today continue to place Black lesbians in butch roles because of this racial stereotype.

In the 1950s and 60s dyke was used in the lesbian subculture as a word for a butch. Since the 1980s it has been used as a positive word for a lesbian who is stroppy, independent and strong or a lesbian with politics. Some lesbians believe that dyke is a word that originated in Greek mythology and once meant hermaphrodite.

I prefer dyke to lesbian. Lesbian is attached to Lesbos, and certainly Lesbos wasn't the beginning of lesbians. Dyke isn't a Eurocentric word, it is not attached to a place in Europe. Aqeela Alam

If I feel in a ragga or swagger mood I may call myself a dyke. Araba Mercer

Dyke for me is about being strong and difficult. I use it among men. Femi Otitoju

Gay

Gay is derived from the Middle French term *gai*. In the fifteenth and sixteenth centuries it was a word used in British theatre to describe female characters (played by men) who were saucy and sexually promiscuous. During the nineteenth century it became a term for women and men who were different from the norm. In the 1920s and 30s it was adopted by homosexual men to describe themselves.

In the late 1960s and early 70s gay was the term chosen by homosexual women and men organising together politically, as in the Gay Liberation Front in Britain. It has now become the standard word for a homosexual, used by heterosexuals and homosexuals alike. During the past decade gay has increasingly come to refer only to homosexual men, and 'lesbian and' is added if women are included. Many Black lesbians see the term as meaning both White and male.

Gay to me means White men with handlebar moustaches, white t-shirts, tight jeans, swinging leather jackets at Gay Pride. Dorothea Smartt

I use gay when I'm talking to my cousins. Marlene Bogle

Gay is a term that I believe grew out of the Stonewall riots in New York in 1969, when drag queens were fighting back against the police. These White genderfuckers have nothing to do with me. Femi Otitoju

Queer

Queer originally meant strange and odd, crooked, not straight. In the early twentieth century it was a term of abuse for homosexuals.

During the late 1980s queer was reclaimed by American lesbians and gay men as a term of self-definition. Queer politics – typified by activist groups such as ACT UP and Queer Nation – developed out of a predominantly White North American experience of anger that the strategy of gay assimilation into mainstream society had still failed to win basic rights. The queer movement believes that women and men should organise together to promote an 'up front, in yer face' sexual politics aimed at upsetting the straight world and sometimes other lesbians and gay men. Queer has also been adopted as an intellectual position by some lesbian and gay writers and academics.

Queer can be used as a loose term to embrace people of different sexual orientations and perversions. The queer 'scene' has provided an opportunity for some lesbians to experiment sexually – to go out 'packing' for the night with a strap-on dildo, and to cruise gay men. The queer debate is probably understood by few lesbians in Britain and some Black lesbians believe it has nothing to do with them.

Queer feels very White to me. It feels too trendy, and trendy terms come and go. Jackie Kay

Queer is a new generation. I associate it with SM. Dorothea Smartt

Queer means people walking around saying: what's that, can I fuck it? Will it fuck me? Queer people are in a different place from me. I'm not on the edge of society. Femi Otitoju

I have no problem with queer – I call myself bent, pervert, lesbian or dyke. The problem is with the people who try to attack me with these words.
Linda Bellos

Feminist

A feminist is someone who struggles for women's rights and believes in the equality of the sexes. It could be argued that there have been feminists since women and men have been on earth. Women such as the Jewish leader Deborah, Boadicea, Cleopatra and Joan of Arc, all of whom broke away from traditional models of female behaviour, could be counted as early examples.

The most recent wave of feminism in Britain and the US began in the 1960s and 70s. The movement was dominated by White women who seemed to think that all the problems women experience are caused by patriarchy, ignoring racism. In the 1980s Black women in Britain reclaimed the term feminist and redefined feminism to include issues of race, class, gender, sexuality and imperialism. They acknowledged the efforts of the long line of Black women before them who had negotiated their way through White western culture.

Defining ourselves as feminists, however means that we have placed ourselves in the front line to fight oppression and exploitation in the systematic ways in which they deny us power and control over our lives – racism, imperialism, class and male supremacy.
'We Are Here: Black Feminist Newsletter', Issue 10, 1986

In our countries of origin there are long traditions of feminists who have struggled against different forms of patriarchy. So the term feminist will mean different things to women of different backgrounds.

I call myself feminist. I don't subscribe to the argument that feminist is a White woman's word. Araba Mercer

Feminism is a major way I find to explain and analyse the world. Despite arguments I've had with other Black women about how feminism has been very White and often betrayed Black women, I still call myself a feminist.
B: England P: Guyana/Ireland (QR)

I use feminist out of habit and laziness. Most people know what it means. But feminism still is a White western ideology and still can't treat Black women as worthy of being at the centre of the debate.
B: Trinidad and Tobago P: Jamaica/Trinidad (QR)

I understand the feminist revolution to be a White middle-class movement that failed to take on issues of race. B: England P: Nigeria (QR)

A Black woman is not a feminist, she is a tireless phenomenon in a White-dominated racist society. B: England P: Jamaica (QR)

Womanist

'Womanist is to feminist as purple is to lavender,' wrote the Black American novelist Alice Walker in *In Search of our Mothers' Gardens*. Walker describes a womanist as a woman who loves other women sexually or non-sexually, prefers female culture, is spiritual, loves music, food, and herself. Womanist can mean a Black feminist and is more widely used in the US than in Britain.

Feminist is outdated, now Black women are calling themselves womanist. Marlene Bogle

Womanist at least addresses the issues of race and class.
B: London P: Nigeria (QR)

At one point there was a discussion about whether you should call yourself a feminist or a womanist. Basically terms need to be simplified because you wouldn't understand what womanist meant unless you'd read certain books. Anne Hayfield

Some women use womanist when they feel that they're into feminism but don't like the word feminist because it sounds too militant. Hope Massiah

Race versus sexuality

It is inevitable that Black lesbians from different backgrounds will choose different names to define themselves. Our experiences are rich, vibrant and diverse; it would be ludicrous to think there could be only one right term for us. Labels are fluid: some Black lesbians have their own names in their own cultures and other words for their families or other parts of the lesbian and gay world. Race, class and cultural and social influences all play a part in each individual's choice of which term suits her best, as does the situation in which she finds herself. There are also particular and legitimate issues like racism and discrimination which affect our lives as Black women. Prefixes such as Black or the names of the countries from which we originate are necessary to acknowledge and validate these experiences.

Pressure in the lesbian world for individuals to define themselves and their political allegiances on the basis of sexuality alone has sometimes meant that Black women feel forced to choose between their sexuality and race. For many Black lesbians, sexuality and race cannot be separated, both are integral components of their identity. Others believe that race is more important, either because it is more visible or because it is made invisible by both the heterosexual and homosexual world and needs to be affirmed or stated. To refer to either our sexuality or our race is not enough when speaking about Black lesbian lives.

My sexuality and race are both important, because the forces that subjugate me as a lesbian are the same as those which oppress me as a Black woman. Sometimes I am more vocal as a lesbian, at other times I am more vocal about my Blackness.
B: Trinidad and Tobago P: Jamaica/Trinidad (QR)

Although my sexuality is an integral part of myself, my race in general is more significant. Linda Bellos

At the moment race is more important because global issues of violence and poverty are important. When you first Come Out sexuality is often the most important thing. Araba Mercer

Most of the time my race is the issue, because as a dark-skinned African-Caribbean woman it is the most obvious thing about me. My sexuality becomes an issue when I'm around Black people. Dorothea Smartt

To me what is important is to be a woman and lesbian in Britain. I would associate myself with the lesbian community rather than with the Chinese one. B: Hong Kong P: China (LHIC)

My sex and race go hand in hand. I couldn't begin to separate one from the other, because the heterosexism in this society compounds the racism I face from day to day... If any one part of me is not provided for, either my sexuality or race, I can't be happy. Femi Otitoju

My race is where I've come from, my heritage, my history; my sexuality is who I am and my individuality. I can't live with just one of these. B: England P: Cyprus (QR)

Racism in the margins

❝ *Racism. The belief in the inherent superiority of one race over all others and thereby the right to dominance, manifest and implied.* ❞ Audre Lorde, 'Sister Outsider', The Crossing Press/Trumansburg, New York, 1984, p.124

❝ *To say that racism is our problem is out and out racism.* ❞
B: England P: Sierra Leone/St Kitts (QR)

All White people are racist because they are socialised by western societies riddled with prejudice and ignorance. This is perpetuated through continual police harassment and immigration control of Black people and reinforced by negative images in everyday life. For example on television Black people are portrayed as living in extreme poverty in Africa and India; in the press we are immigrants flooding into Britain for refuge; to some people we are responsible for the shortage of jobs and council houses. The majority of positive role models in British society are White and many of the negative role models are Black. Children in British schools learn that White people civilised and discovered Africa, the Caribbean, America and Australia.

I have had a lot of problems with the police... I get stopped to check my licence and when they realise that I'm a foreigner, they treat me really badly. They want to see my passport, they want to know what I'm doing in this country, whether I have proper residency, nothing to do with my driving. Once... they had me in there for two hours just showing my licence. B: Iran P: Iran (LHIC)

Many White lesbians come into intimate contact with Black women for the first time in the lesbian community; any contact they have had before may well have been shrouded with racism, fear, distrust or suspicion. Yet few White women are prepared to discuss or even acknowledge these issues and fewer still are prepared to confront their own racism. They either believe it is not their problem or are too afraid to talk about it.

White lesbians often say: let's all be comfortable together and let it all be nice and not too difficult. They conveniently ignore that we are different, and that we have a different experience. Femi Otitoju

My gripe with White lesbians is that they believe we are all homosexuals together, and tend not to want to discuss the issue of race and their own racism. Marlene Bogle

Black lesbians are often patronised by White lesbians who feel so guilty and so afraid of us that they never contradict us. Linda Bellos

Lesbian and gay institutions

It is no surprise that the national lesbian and gay press is owned by White gay men. *The Pink Paper, Capital Gay* and *Gay Times* publish very little about lesbians and even less about Black lesbians and gays. None of them currently employs a Black worker on their editorial staff and few of us have worked with any of the lesbian and gay press in the past.

There is often wilful ignorance about our famous Black lesbians. For example, a White lesbian employee from *The Pink Paper* did not know who the Black American lesbian writer Audre Lorde was. When she was informed of her death during November 1992, she replied 'Who is Audre Lorde?' Hope Massiah

Political organisations too have often excluded us. In August 1992 the campaign group OutRage London voted to disband its People of Colour sub-group. Other organisations have rarely considered having such sub-groups. National organisations such as Gay Pride have a poor track record when it comes to involving Black lesbians and gay men at any organisational level. When the London Lesbian and Gay Centre was in existence, with one or two exceptions Black lesbians and gays formed no part of the board of directors, management, paid workers or volunteers.

When racism is placed on the agenda, some White lesbians and gay men respond with irritation. They seem to think we should prioritise the fight against heterosexism over that against racism. Others perceive Black lesbians and gays as being deliberately difficult when they raise issues of racism or race – their attitude seems to be that it doesn't happen in the lesbian and gay community.

Nightclubs

Some nightclubs in Britain have always had door policies against Black people. Many club owners believe that if Black people frequent their clubs fights will break out and personal property will be stolen. Venues for lesbians are hard to get, and Black women find it doubly difficult to persuade club owners to invest in them.

Yet the level of racism in White-run women-only clubs has hardly changed since the 1960s and Black lesbians throughout Britain have been refused entry because of the colour of their skin or have been granted 'honorary White status' only by arriving in the company of White women. In addition Black women out in lesbian nightclubs may be faced with women wearing fascist regalia or skinheads wearing Union Jacks.

There have been door policies over the years where Black women are not allowed in except with a White woman. Anne Hayfield

During the late 1970s I met this Arab lesbian who was born here... and she had a bruised eye. She had been kicked at a women's bar by some White lesbians who called her a wog and kicked her out. She still has a deaf ear after that, and her spine is still not functioning.
B: Middle East P: Middle East (LHIC)

In 1985 a London club was picketed by a group of Black and White lesbians because it had refused Black women entry. In front of the protesters' eyes, club hosts allowed White women in after Black women had been told the club was full. One Black woman accompanied by some White women was also allowed in.

In 1990 a group of eight Black lesbians out in London's West End after seeing a performance decided to go to a well-known women-only club. When they arrived, they were asked if they were at the right nightclub. After they told the club hosts that they were all lesbians, the hosts replied: 'Sorry, this is a members-only club.'

In 1992 Britain's longest-running weekly women-only club told its two DJs not to play reggae music because it attracted too many Black women. Overheard at a SHAKTI disco (a group run by South Asian lesbians and gays) was the comment: 'Why can't you play proper music instead of that paki music?'

Common scenarios

In Britain Black lesbians and gay men are a minority within the homosexual world. Therefore White lesbians and gay men have often ignored or marginalised our issues in both cultural and political contexts. Every Black lesbian has her own story to tell. What follows are examples of the types of racism that frequently arise.

Racism by omission

White women conduct research about lesbians living in Britain. They compile a book and call it *Lesbians in Britain*. Few references are made to Black women. Their excuse is that they were not able to find any information on Black lesbians.

A lot of racism in the lesbian and gay community is racism by omission and through ignorance. Araba Mercer

Racism by exclusion and tokenism

White lesbians organise a conference in a major city. They panic because none of the local Black women have enrolled. At the eleventh hour they ring a Black woman living in another city and ask if she will come and speak at the conference.

The racism I've experienced is of not acknowledging my presence at a function or event. B: Pakistan P: Pakistan (QR)

We are either excluded, made invisible or used as a token.
B: England P: Cyprus (QR)

As an Out visible lesbian in the media and on the scene during the 1980s, I often experienced racism in the form of tokenism. Whenever I was invited to speak or write about lesbians and gay men, I was always asked to cover the race issues. Femi Otitoju

Racism by invisibility

A White woman is visiting a lesbian organisation. She walks into an office where six workers are seated. The first three women she passes are Black; she ignores them and directs all her enquiries to the three White lesbians. They respond without acknowledging the Black lesbians sitting in the room.

Racism by ignorance and fear

White women are concerned that Black women are not attending the local women's centre. It is explained that if Black women are to feel welcome, the centre should employ at least two Black workers. The White workers panic; they are afraid this could mean losing their own jobs. The management committee reassures them, stating that if the centre receives additional funding, a Black worker will be employed. After a couple of months the subject is forgotten.

Racism by guilt

A group of lesbians are exchanging ideas. A Black woman stands up and says: 'You haven't included us'. The whole room is engulfed in a strained and guilty silence. A White woman rushes to the rescue and offers the Black woman a platform to speak from. No one listens or tries to understand.

Time and time again the same shit comes up, and time and time again the White lesbian will find a way to run and hide from the issue of White racism towards Lesbians of Colour. This poisons relationships.
Anna Juleya Hearne

Racism hurts

The reaction of Black lesbians to the racism they experience in the lesbian and gay community manifests itself internally and externally as anger, pain, frustration and exhaustion. Audre Lorde states in her book *Sister Outsider* that a Black woman's response to racism is anger: anger at exclusion, unquestioned privilege, racial distortion, silence, ill-use, stereotyping, defensiveness, misnaming, betrayal and co-option.

Some Black women active in the lesbian and gay community over a period of many years have given up trying to raise the consciousness of White lesbians: why should they channel their energies into challenging White women, when so many issues between Black lesbians have been ignored? White women sometimes ask: 'Why don't Black lesbians integrate within the lesbian and gay world?' They rarely understand that Black lesbians need environments free of racism. To accuse us of racism when we organise Black-women only conferences, social activities and meeting groups is symptomatic of racism by fear and ignorance.

Talking about racism is asking me to drag up a lot of pain. It is all too exhausting. Linda Bellos

Racism affects Black lesbians from different racial backgrounds in different ways. For example, the European view of Asian people is that they are passive, cute, quiet, sensitive, gentle and submissive. African and African-Caribbean people are perceived as aggressive, boisterous, with a chip on their shoulder, trouble-makers, muggers and good at sports. And these attitudes are just as prevalent in the lesbian and gay communities.

For White people generally, being Asian is something to do with curry, saris, brown skins, funny music, strange religions, something to do with ethnics. Shivanada Khan, 'SHAKTI', vol. 1, April/May 1989

Challenging racism is as important to Black lesbians as challenging heterosexism. But our fight against racism can only be won if the White lesbian and gay communities begin to recognise and talk about racism among themselves and develop strategies to deal with it constructively. Whether overt or covert, racism hurts.

SM politics

The use and abuse of power – sexual, emotional, physical, spiritual – within a relationship is something we have all experienced at some time in our lives. Those lesbians and gays who practise sado-masochism (SM) believe that as consenting adults they can explore and use such power imbalances.

The visible face of SM has caused much anger and debate in lesbian communities in Britain. In the 1980s in London SM lesbians were becoming increasingly apparent and many lesbians angered by SM fashion and practice made strict dress codes a condition for admittance to events to deny entry to lesbians wearing SM clothing – studded leather collars, belts, bracelets and jackets, chains, handcuffs and fascist regalia such as swastikas.

Black lesbians took part in the fierce debates that arose. Along with many White lesbians, they argued that such clothing and behaviour conjured up racist and fascist images connected with slavery and Nazi Germany. They also argued that the notion of lesbians enshrining power imbalances in their relationships was problematic at a time when the issue of racism in the lesbian communities had yet to be effectively addressed.

I was in Women Against Violence Against Women. I argued against SM because it used the symbolism of slavery and violence. Linda Bellos

I don't think SM is necessarily racist. SM exists in all communities. I believe Black lesbians practise SM. Araba Mercer

By 1987 there was such a strong SM lesbian presence that after the Lesbian Strength march two separate social events were organised, one of which had a strict dress code. During the demonstration a group of White SM lesbians surrounded both the Black and Jewish groups, causing the whole march to halt until they had been moved to the back.

In 1988 the London Women's Centre hosted a panel discussion to put forward the arguments for and against SM. It was an attempt to provide a forum for debate, rather than relying on dress codes, exclusion and the presumption that the issues were obvious to resolve the dispute. Black lesbians stayed away; only four were present and any arguments based on the racist connotations of SM were dismissed by the White SM crowd on the grounds that there was one Black lesbian with them. There was no meeting ground: non-SM lesbians were regarded as vanilla, tame, soft, boring and reactionary, while SM lesbians saw themselves as sexual pioneers pushing back the boundaries of sexuality.

The late 1980s saw the establishment in London of the first successful lesbian SM club. In protest, a number of Black and White lesbians attempted to demolish the building with hammers and pick-axes. Although some damage was caused, the club remained in business.

In 1989, the first issue of *Quim*, a quarterly lesbian magazine, was published. It aimed to 'talk about and celebrate what makes us lesbians – our sex with women.' The first issue included a story depicting sexual abuse of children and images of White women with shaved heads in leather, chains, studs and uniforms. 1989 was also the year Sheba Feminist Publishers launched its popular book *Serious Pleasure*, an anthology of 'lesbian erotica'. Sheba was accused of being pornographers on the basis that the stories included so-called lesbian sexual fantasies of anonymous sex and sex with a 15-year-old girl.

There were rumours that Sheba was funded by *Penthouse*. I landed myself with a reputation in the Black lesbian community as an outrageous SM dyke, which I'm not. Araba Mercer

While there has been no organised Black SM lesbian scene in Britain, some Black lesbians do practise SM, either through involvement in the White scene or in their own homes. Over the years attitudes have changed.

I used to be horrified by SM. But over the years I've come round to thinking that what two people do behind closed doors in their bedroom is up to them. Marlene Bogle

The arguments about SM in the lesbian community have masked the need for safe, open debates about lesbian sex and sexuality. Too many discussions have been polarised along the line of where individuals stood regarding SM, with no space to talk about the realities of lesbian sex in a way that includes the fact that it is not always a glorious experience. Neither has there been room to discuss the fact that lesbians can and do abuse each other in ways that have nothing to do with consent.

The way the issue of whether one is pro or anti SM has been institutionalised in the lesbian and gay movement is an artificial dialogue. SM is a camouflage issue that disguises the real issues of sexuality and power abuse. Anna Juleya Hearne

Black lesbians need to create a space where we can discuss these issues openly and generously – a space where we do not feel silenced because sex is traumatic for us, because we have been emotionally or physically abused as children or adults by family members, strangers or lovers, because we practise SM. Our sexuality and sexual practice should not be concerned with scoring points for being radical or right-on, but with understanding the complexities of our whole experiences.

Fast-forward

Much has changed since 1981. Delegates of the third OWAAD conference were astounded when 40 women got up to join the lesbian workshop. There are now more Black lesbians than ever visible on the lesbian scene throughout the country. Our increased presence has prompted a growing awareness in lesbian and gay clubs and at benefit events of Black musical traditions: soul, jazz, reggae, bhangra and other Black music. There has also been an increase in the number of Out Black lesbian writers and performers. Black lesbians have challenged the visual stereotypes of what a lesbian looks like through our different appearances and cultural fashions.

Sadly, Black lesbians have been affected by the increased unemployment and homelessness, rising cuts in welfare benefits and attacks on health, education and social services which have characterised the past decade and a half of Conservative rule. The feeling of optimism and faith in the possibility of real political change has waned as successive legislative measures curbing the rights of all marginalised people have been passed. The Police and Criminal Evidence and Prevention of Terrorism Acts increased police powers. Various immigration regulations denied families the right to be together and others the right to a safe haven. Successive government acts have limited expenditure by local councils, leading to cuts in local equalities initiatives. All of these have fed the growth of racist, homophobic and misogynist violence. A widespread feeling of disillusion and despair has led to a 'fuck politics, let's party' attitude which is apparent in all communities, including among Black lesbians.

Years of Thatcherism and now Major have killed a lot of people's spirits. It has made people very apathetic, selfish and self-obsessed. The whole community has been devastated... and we're just a part of that and it's so sad. Jackie Kay

We depended on the Greater London Council and other council funding for our groups' activities. Now that's dissolved, we are scurrying around like headless chickens with no solid strategies for creating and setting a movement's focus. B: Trinidad and Tobago P: Jamaica/Trinidad (QR)

There were more women's centres and Black groups around to support women when I Came Out. Today there is only a social scene for new

dykes. There is no political debate. I believe we have become fragmented, people are into enjoying their sexuality through parties. Marlene Bogle

There seemed to be so much more going on in the 1980s, everything was new, things were possible. There was so much dialogue and political theorising. Today there are just parties and literary events. Araba Mercer

In attempting to establish a sense of our identity, Black lesbians encounter discrimination from all sides. So many people refuse to accept us as 'whole': Black, lesbian, born here, born overseas, woman, feminist, mother, carer, disabled, older, and so on. Racism in the wider lesbian and gay communities is on the increase, there is homophobia in the Black communities and our families, and woman-hating attitudes are rife. Few places are safe for us. The cost to our health – emotional, physical and spiritual – is severe. Alcohol and drug abuse are high and support for those coming to terms with their addictions is low.

For many of us the ideal is to be among other Black lesbians – a safe haven, a home, a place where we can be accepted in our entirety. But while the potential is vast, the reality can be painful as our fears of being hurt and rejected by other Black lesbians turn to distrust and hostility. While such barriers remain, it seems impossible to create spaces for all of us. There are no groups for Black lesbians with disabilities and only a few for older or younger Black lesbians. And there are none that bring us all together.

Relating to other Black lesbians brings out your whole feelings about how you feel in the world, how you're excluded in the world, how you're betrayed in the world. Aqeela Alam

There are a lot of Black lesbians out smiling and having a good time, but on the quiet they are experiencing a painful time. Pain is something we need to talk about, we need to find ways in which we can support each other. Hope Massiah

Suspicion and distrust of each other has created these tiny factions... jealousies, insecurities and paranoia, all the things that are results of being oppressed. Jackie Kay

Our movement is wrecked, on the rocks and bleeding to death. But most people seem quite happy to pretend it's all still working. Anna Juleya Hearne

Organising for the future

There are many issues we need to tackle urgently. And there are our visions and dreams to realise, both for ourselves and for each other. All require us to organise and work together and in coalitions with others, both creatively and systematically.

Since Black lesbians are present in all sections of the community, we need to have our issues incorporated into all community struggles for justice and basic standards of living and service delivery, whether in health care, housing, immigration. Savitri Hensman

The crux of the matter is what sort of abuses each person, each community is facing, and what are we doing about it and how are we working on it in a way that encompasses everyone, including those who have recently arrived in this country. Aqeela Alam

There are many issues to do with health and ageing that we, alongside other lesbians, should be addressing. HIV/AIDS, sickle-cell, cervical and breast cancer are some of these. We have to establish forums where we can share experiences and information.

I worry about getting older, and if we should be so ill that we have to go into supervised care with all those heterosexual women. What's going to happen then? We should be organising a retirement home for that time. Some women from the Older Lesbian Network started the Rock October Trust, to set up retirement homes. But it should be something lesbians of all ages are involved in. Marie

In order to fight for our survival as a visible, organised presence and to realise our dreams and visions, we need to start loving and caring for ourselves. Not as an end in itself, but as a means to create a true sense of community

We need to work on issues of identity as a community. At the moment we're very divided. Unless we come to terms with this identity crisis we are going to disappear as an entity. Teresa Hope

We need to look at how we have avoided each other for so long and failed, in the main, to provide real support or friendship for ourselves and each other. Zehra

Let's get together under Lesbians of Colour and start to build a real 'home' for each other. B: England P: Germany/India (QR)

We have to find pride in ourselves and our heritage, positive thinking with regard to our sexuality, understanding towards and support for each other. B: W. Indies P: W. Indies (QR)

We need to look at the different types of racism people experience and what these mean to us individually and collectively. Zehra

We've got to find ways of securing some sort of economic base for ourselves, which could mean a lot of women getting together to share skills or setting up co-ops. Anne Hayfield

We should be producing high-quality materials for consumption by Black lesbians. B: Britain P: Nigeria (QR)

We should have greater networking throughout the country.
B: England P: Zanzibar/England (QR)

If women earning well were prepared to invest, we could start to publish our thoughts, start art galleries, coffee shops, sustainable Black lesbian projects. B: England P: Sierra Leone/St Kitts (QR)

A holiday home would be nice, where Black lesbians could go and spend a weekend, somewhere in this country for people who can't afford a holiday.
Marie

I think we need to sort ourselves out first, get some sense of unity and then deal with the world. Quickly. B: England P: India (QR)

Our movement can be salvaged by a level of self-love and honesty, a willingness to open to what it means to love the female, love nature, love a Woman of Colour. Even if that first means confessing how much we loathe it.
Anna Juleya Hearne

Truth is like a gigantic jigsaw in which each individual's experiences contribute to the whole picture. No one individual, community, religion or set of politics has a monopoly on truth.

To build a solid Black lesbian community with a greater feeling of unity, we must allow each Black lesbian a space to express the truth of her experiences. If that challenges our assumptions, contradicts our norms, then perhaps we should consider whether these need to be changed or dropped altogether rather than automatically assuming that it is the other woman who is wrong. If we as Black lesbians are to learn from the collective identity crisis we find ourselves in, we need to create this space for ourselves and one another and in the process begin to build a self-confident, vibrant, welcoming community.

Black lesbians in Britain will always be here, Out or closeted. We are the pioneers of our own future.

Now and then: a Black lesbian chronology

This chronology charts the rise, and in some cases the fall, of those organisations, conferences and publications in Britain with a strong Black lesbian input. It is not complete, because there is no one archive that has systematically kept records of all our history. This chronology has been put together by trawling through the Lesbian Archives, the Feminist Library and the Black Lesbian and Gay Centre. All of them face threats to their future. The other part of this research came from our own and other people's memories.

1978
Brixton Black Women's Group (London) takes up the idea of establishing a Black Women's Centre in London.
February Organisation of Women of Africa and African Descent (OWAAD) launched as an umbrella national Black group.
Winter OWAAD becomes Organisation of Women of African and Asian Descent. Folded 1982. First conference attended by 250 women.

1979
July *FOWAAD* (OWAAD newsletter) first issue.
Brixton Black Women's Centre (London). Folded due to funding cuts in 1986 and because the building was condemned.
Southall Black Sisters (London) formed by women of Asian and African descent.

1980
OWAAD second conference held over two days and attended by 600 women.

1981
Gay Asian Group becomes Gay Black Group (London). Later becomes Lesbian and Gay Black Group and founds Black Lesbian and Gay Centre project.
Peckham Black Women's Group (London) formed to include women of African and Asian descent; later sets up a centre. Folded due to loss of funding in 1990.

OWAAD third annual conference (London). 40 Black lesbians gather for the first lesbian workshop. The conference is divided over the issue of lesbianism.

1982
Black Lesbian Group, Britain's first. Although meetings happen in London, lesbians from all over the country attend. Folded.

March *Outwrite Women's Newspaper* first issue. Folded 1989.

June OWAAD last conference attempts to bring women together with the focus on Black feminism. OWAAD folds.

1983
Black Women Talk, a group of women of African and Asian descent, comes together to form a publishing co-operative.

Chinese Lesbian Group launched after three lesbians meet at the Lesbian Sex and Sexual Practice conference.

Black Lesbian Support Network, national network acting as a contact point for women. Folded 1986/7.

1984
Asian Women's Writers Collective provides support to new writers, skill-sharing, performances and outreach.

Black Women's Discos held monthly at South London Women's Centre. Folded.

April Black Women and Media national conference (London); practical skill-sharing and discussion forum.

Spring *Mukti* Asian feminist magazine first issue. Folded.

May We Are Here: Black Feminists in Britain national conference (London) attended by 250 women.

June First International Feminist Bookfair. Barbara Burford, Audre Lorde and Suniti Namjoshi discuss their writings.

July *We Are Here: Black Feminist Newsletter* first issue. Folded 1986.

Autumn *Feminist Review* publishes 'Many Voices, One Chant: Black Feminist Perspectives' (No. 17). It includes a discussion between four Black lesbians.

Mid 1980s
Camden Black Lesbian Group (London) joins with Camden Lesbian Project.

Latin American Lesbian Group (London).

1985
September Black Lesbian Group (London) meets at Waltham Forest Women's Centre. Folded.

LESPOP (Lesbians and Policing Project) (London) gives advice, information

and runs workshops. Folded due to loss of funding in 1990.
October Zami I first national Black lesbian conference (London) attended by over 200 women of African and Asian descent.
Zami Black feminist bi-monthly magazine (Coventry) first issue. Folded.
Black Lesbian and Gay Centre Project (London) gains mainstream funding to establish a centre.
Peckham Black Women's Centre (London). Folded 1990.
'Lesbians from Historically Immigrant Communities', research by a Black lesbian of Turkish descent funded by the Greater London Council.
Lesbian and Gay Immigration Group established from work by Black lesbian conducting LHIC research. Folded due to burn-out 1990.
BLASIA (London) group for Black lesbians of Asian descent. Folded.

1986
April Camden Lesbian Centre/Black Lesbian Group (London) granted planning permission for the country's first lesbian centre.
April Lesbian and Gay Unit, the first in the country, set up in Haringey (London) and employs Black lesbian workers.

1987
March Challenging Heterosexism in Our Communities conference (London) co-organised by Black Lesbian and Gay Centre.
May Smash the Backlash national demonstration (London) against homophobic and racist attitudes/actions. 4,000 march.
June Black Women Talk publishes its first book, *Black Women Talk Poetry*.
Black Lesbian and Gay Group (Leicester).
Cypriot Lesbian and Gay Group (London).

1988
We Are Here: Black Feminist Newsletter (Leicester) relaunched. Folded 1989.
Shakti network (London) for South Asian lesbians, gays and bisexuals.
Black Lesbians and Gay People of Faith (London) as a space for those from any religion. Folded 1990.
African/Caribbean Lesbian Group (London). Folded 1990.

1989
April Zami II second national Black lesbian conference (Birmingham) held over two days and attended by over 200 women.
Light-skinned/mixed-race Black lesbian group (London) formed after a workshop at Zami II. Later formed MOSAIC (1991).
Black Lesbians Brought Up In Care Group (London). Folded.

International Black Lesbians Group to offer support to and from those born overseas. Folded 1990.

Black Lesbian Group (Birmingham).

Late 1980s

Women in Shakti (London).

Young Black Zamis (London), part of youth project North London Line. Folded 1990.

Onyx (London), group for lesbians of Colour. Folded early 1990s.

Young Black Lesbian Group (London) formed as part of Lewisham Young Women's Project.

Over 40s Black Lesbian Group (London).

Zamimass (London) set up initially to organise an alternative Xmas celebration, continued as a monthly group.

1990

Orientations group for lesbians and gays of Chinese and South East Asian descent (London).

Sixth International Lesbian and Gay People of Colour Conference (London) attended by 300 people from all over the world.

1991

Black Lesbian Group (Nottingham).

Black Lesbian and Gay Group (Manchester).

Black Lesbian and Gay Helpline, open one night a week.

MOSAIC for lesbians and gay men of mixed racial heritage (London).

1992

September Northern Black Lesbian conference (Manchester) attended by over 100 women.

November Black Lesbian, Gay and Bisexual Group (Bristol).

1993

March Zami Network International Women's Day Festival (Birmingham) day of workshops and discussions.

MOSAIC conference for lesbians and gays of mixed racial heritage (London).

Iranian Lesbian and Gay Group (London).

Resources

Groups and Contacts

Birmingham
Black Lesbian and Gay Group (Kola) Tel: Friend 021 622 7351
Shakti (South Asian lesbian and gay network) Tel: 021 622 7351
Zami Network c/o Birmingham Women's Workshops, Unit 9, Whitworth Industrial Park, Tilton Road, Small Heath, Birmingham B9 4PE

Bradford
Shakti Tel: 0274 723802/722206

Bristol
Black Lesbian, Gay and Bisexual Group (Safar) Tel: 0272 425927

Leeds
Black Lesbian Support Group c/o Harehills Housing Aid, 188 Roundhay Road, Harehills, Leeds 8

London
Black Lesbians And Gays Against Media Homophobia (BLAGAMH) FREEPOST, London SE8 5BR Tel: Ted 081 692 1308
Black Lesbian, Gay and Bisexual Group (16 to 25-year-olds) The Old Laundry, Hornsey Road, London N7 7QT Tel: 071 281 2121/272 8467
Black Lesbian and Gay Centre (BLGC) BM Box 4390, London WC1N 3XX Tel: 071 732 3885
Black Lesbian and Gay Helpline (Thurs 7-10pm) Tel: 071 837 5364
Black Lesbian Cultural Workers Collective Tel: 071 732 3885 (for information)
Black Lesbians in Solidarity PO Box 11, 124 Vassall Road, London SW9 6JB
Camden Black Lesbian Group CLC/BLG, 54-56 Phoenix Road, London NW1 1ES Tel: 071 383 5405
Cypriot Lesbian and Gay Group c/o London Friend, 86 Caledonian Road, London N1 Tel: 071 837 2782
Iranian Lesbian and Gay Group c/o London Friend, 86 Caledonian Road, London N1 Tel: 071 837 2782
Las Divinas (Latin American Lesbian Group) c/o CLC/BLG, 54-56 Phoenix Road,

London NW1 1ES Tel: 071 383 5405
Older Black Lesbian Group (Over 40s) c/o West Hampstead Women's Centre, 55 Hempstel Road, London NW6 Tel: 071 328 7389
Orientations (Chinese and South East Asian Lesbian and Gay Group) c/o London Friend, 86 Caledonian Road, London N1 Tel: 071 837 2782
Shakti (South Asian lesbian and gay network) c/o London Friend, 86 Caledonian Road, London N1 Tel: 071 837 2782
Young Black Lesbian Group c/o Lewisham Young Women's Project, 308 Brownhill Road, London SE6 1AU Tel: 081 698 6675
Zamimass (Working Class Lesbian Group) c/o CLC/BLG, 54-56 Pheonix Road, London NW1 1ES Tel: 071 383 5405

Manchester
Black Lesbian and Gay Group PO Box 153, Manchester M60 1LP
Black Lesbian Support Group c/o Box No. 26, 1 Newton Street, Piccadilly, Manchester M1 1HW
Black Lesbian Writing Group c/o Box No. 26, 1 Newton Street, Piccadilly, Manchester M1 1HW
Zami (Young Black Lesbian Group) Tel: 061 834 7256/ 236 6205

Further reading

The following books include fiction and non-fiction, poetry, prose and photographs by or about Black lesbians in Britain.

Amos, Valerie, Lewis, Gail, Mama, Amina, Parmar, Pratibha eds., *Feminist Review*, 'Many Voices, One Chant: Black Feminist Perspectives', London No.17, Autumn 1984.

Bang, Mary Jo ed., *Whatever You Desire*, London, The Oscars Press, 1990.

Bishop, Jacky, Livia, Anna, Mohin, Lilian eds., *Gossip* Nos.2 and 5, A Journal of Lesbian Feminist Ethics, London, Onlywomen Press, 1986.

Boffin, Tessa, Fraser, Jean eds., *Stolen Glances: Lesbians Take Photographs*, London, Pandora, 1991.

Burford, Barbara, *The Threshing Floor*, London, Sheba Feminist Publishers, 1986.

Burford, Barbara, Kay, Jackie, Nichols, Grace, Pearse, Gabriela, *A Dangerous Knowing: Four Black Women Poets*, London, Sheba Feminist Publishers, Undated.

Burford, Barbara, Macrae, Lindsay, Paskin, Sylvia eds., *Dancing the Tightrope – New Love Poems by Women*, London, The Women's Press, 1987.

Cant, Bob, Hemmings, Susan eds., *Radical Records: 30 Years of Lesbian and Gay History 1957-1987*, London, Routledge, 1988.

Choong, Da, Cole-Wilson, Olivette, Evaristo, Bernadine, Pearse, Gabriela eds., *Black Women Talk Poetry*, London, Black Women Talk, 1987.

Chowdry, Maya, Janjua, Shiadah, Seneviratne, *Putting in the pickle where the jam should be*, Sheffield, Write Back/Jag Rahi Hai, 1989.

Dupont, D., Fletcher, F., Lohoni, D. eds., *Listen My Sister – Putting AIDS into Context*, London, South East London Commissioning Agency, 1992.

Grewal, Shabnam, et al eds., *Charting the Journey: Writings by Black and Third World Women*, London, Sheba Feminist Publishers, 1988.

Hall Carpenter Archives, Lesbian Oral History Group, *Inventing Ourselves: Lesbian Life Stories*, London, Routledge, 1989.

Halpin, Bernadette, Smartt, Dorothea eds., *Words from the Word Up Cafe: Lesbian Poetry from 'Word Up'*, London, Centerprise Publications, 1993.

Hayfield, Anne, *The Issues: Black Lesbians and Black Gay Men*, London, LAGER, 1993.

Hobby, Elaine, White, Chris eds., *What Lesbians Do in Books*, London, The Women's Press, 1991.

Jin, Meiling, *Gifts from My Grandmother*, London, Sheba Feminist Publishers, Undated.

Kaufmann, Tara, Lincoln, Paul eds., *High Risk Lives*, London, Prism Press, 1991.

Kay, Jackie, *Other Lovers*, Newcastle Upon Tyne, Bloodaxe Books, 1993.

Kay, Jackie, *The Adoption Papers*, Newcastle Upon Tyne, Bloodaxe Books, 1991.

Khan, Shivananda, *Khush: A Shakti Report* (South Asian Lesbian and Gay Network), London, Undated.

Livia, Anna, Mohin, Lilian eds., *The Pied Piper: Lesbian Feminist Fiction*, London, Onlywomen Press, 1989.

McEwan, Christine, O'Sullivan, Sue eds., *Naming the Waves: Contemporary Lesbian Poetry*, London, Virago, 1988.

McEwan, Christine, O'Sullivan, Sue eds., *Out the Other Side: Contemporary Lesbian Writing*, London, Virago, 1988.

Mohin, Lilian, ed., *Beautiful Barbarians: Lesbian Feminist Poetry*, London, Onlywomen Press, 1986.

Neild, Suzanne, Pearson, Rosalind eds., *Women Like Us*, London, The Women's Press, 1992.

O'Sullivan, Sue ed., *Turning The Tables: Recipes and Reflections from Women*, London, Sheba Feminist Publishers, 1987.

O'Sullivan, Sue, Parmar, Pratibha, *Lesbians Talk (Safer) Sex*, London, Scarlet Press, 1992.

Smyth, Cherry, *Lesbians Talk Queer Notions*, London, Scarlet Press, 1992.

Sulter, Maud, *As A Black Woman: Poems 1982-1985*, West Yorkshire, Urban Fox Press, 1985.

Sulter, Maud ed., *Passion: A Discourse on Black Women's Creativity*, West Yorkshire, Urban Fox Press, 1990.

Sulter, Maud, *Zabat: Politics of A Family Tree, Poems 1986-1989*, West Yorkshire, Urban Fox Press, 1989.

Film and video

A Prayer Before Birth, Dir. Jacqui Duckworth, 20 mins 1991 (GB). A drama based on the director's experience of coming to terms with multiple sclerosis. Available from Out on a Limb, 071 498 9643

Clause and Effect, 20th Century Vixen, 20 mins 1988 (GB). Looks at the origins and impact of Clause 28 of the Local Government Act 1988. Available from Out on a Limb, 071 498 9643

Framed Youth: Revenge of the Teenage Perverts, Lesbian and Gay Video Project, 45 mins 1983 (GB). Using a wide range of visual material, interviews and music looks at the experiences of young lesbians and gay men in Britain. Available from Out on a Limb, 071 498 9643

How Can I Ignore the Girl Next Door?, Hammersmith and Fulham Young Lesbian Group, 35 mins 1987 (GB). Soap-style drama by a group of young lesbians. Available from Out on a Limb, 071 498 9643

In The Out Tray, Converse Pictures, 2 programmes, 30 mins each 1986 (GB). Addresses lesbian and gay employment rights by looking at discrimination and work being done to combat it. Available from Out on a Limb, 071 498 9643

Khush, Dir. Pratibha Parmar, 24 mins 1991 (GB). Through interviews looks at the issues affecting South Asian lesbians and gay men around the world. Available from Cinenova, 081 981 6828

Memory Pictures, Dir. Pratibha Parmar, 24 mins 1989 (GB). Explores the experience of colonisation, migration, racism and the search for history and identity. Available from Out on a Limb, 071 498 9643

Nocturne, Dir. Joy Chamberlain, 60 mins (GB). A television drama about two runaways who reawaken the hidden desires of a middle-aged woman. Available from Maya Vision, 071 836 1113

Out of Order, West London Media Workshop, 21 mins 1988 (GB). A protest, consisting of interviews and archive footage, against Section 28 of the Local Government Act 1988. Available from Out on a Limb, 071 498 9643

Reframing AIDS, Converse Pictures/Pratibha Parmar, 36 mins 1988 (GB). Uses interviews with a wide spectrum of individuals to challenge the myths and examine the social and political problems AIDS has created for lesbians and gays. Available from Out on a Limb, 071 498 9643

Running Gay, Sheffield Film Co-op, 20 mins 1991 (GB). Why do we need a Gay Games? Documentary about lesbian and gay sportspeople. Available from Out on a Limb, 071 498 9643

The Front Door, Colin Richardson/West London Media Workshop, 11 mins 1989 (GB). Discover how sexuality can never be a private matter. Available from Out on a Limb, 071 498 9643

The Mark of Lilith, Dir. Isling Mack-Nataf/ReVamp Productions, 32 mins 1986 (GB). A mythical love story about a female vampire. Available from Out on a Limb, 071 498 9643

The Passion Of Remembrance, Sankofa, 80 mins 1986 (GB). Innovative drama about the Black experience in Britain, fighting racism outside and conservatism inside. Available from Out on a Limb, 071 498 9643

Women Like Us, Clio Co-op, 55 mins 1989 (GB). Sixteen lesbians aged from 50 to 80 talk about their lives and experiences. Available from Out on a Limb, 071 498 9643

Out from Scarlet Press

Lesbians Talk Queer Notions
Cherry Smyth
What is queer politics? Does the new defiance signify a meaningful shift in ideology, or is it merely wishful thinking on the part of a few white gay men? Are queer politics and feminism in any way compatible? What does queer mean for lesbians, and who is setting the agenda? Cherry Smyth describes the development of the new politics and discusses its implications with an international group of activists and their critics.
ISBN 1 85727 025 8

Lesbians Talk (Safer) Sex
Sue O'Sullivan and Pratibha Parmar
The need for safer sex has revolutionised sexual practice and its discussion within the gay male community and produced a series of hotly contested debates among lesbians which run far deeper than the issue of safer sex itself. Do lesbians need to think about safer sex at all? What has discussion of safer sex revealed about lesbian sexual practices? What research has been done on woman-to-woman transmission? Are lesbian AIDS activists merely servicing gay men or can we formulate a common agenda?
ISBN 1 85727 020 7

The Lesbians Talk Issues series
Lesbian politics in the 1990s has produced a fast-changing agenda of issues and debates, contradictions and differences of opinion. The *Lesbians Talk Issues* series is designed to provide a forum in which topics of current interest within the international lesbian community can be dissected and discussed with immediacy and flexibility.

If you would like to write a pamphlet in response to any of the issues raised in **Lesbians Talk Making Black Waves** *or on any other topical area of lesbian debate, please write to Scarlet Press, 5 Montague Road, London E8 2HN.*